Source code

The source code is available on the authors' website

https://books.abdelfattah-ragab.com

Introduction

Welcome to the book "Angular Portfolio App Development: Create Your Personal Brand". In this book, I explain how to use Angular to create an online portfolio. An online portfolio can help you show the world your skills and impress your employers. It's also a good step towards building your personal brand.

By the end of this book, you will be confident working with Angular and have your own online portfolio.

Let's get started!

PREMIUM QUALITY
SATISFACTION GUARANTEED
Angular
PORT FOLIO
App Development
CREATE YOUR PERSONAL BRAND
Abdelfattah Ragab

Angular Portfolio App Development

Create your personal brand

Abdelfattah Ragab

Chapter 1: Project Preview

1.1 Pages

The project contains the following pages:

- Home
- About
- CV
- Projects
- Contact

1.2 Preview (Mobile)

About

I am Abdelfattah Ragab, a Senior Software Developer with extensive experience of over 20 years in the field. My expertise lies in frontend technologies, with a particular focus on the Angular framework.

Throughout my career, I have honed my skills and knowledge to become proficient in creating exceptional user interfaces and crafting seamless web experiences. My passion for frontend development drives me to stay up-to-date with the latest tools and techniques, enabling me to deliver high-quality solutions to complex problems.

With a proven track record of successful projects, I am recognized for my professionalism, attention to detail, and commitment to achieving outstanding results.

CV

Senior Software Developer - Angular

2019 - Present

Working for clients online:

- Lead Angular teams
- Perform application analysis
- Create architecture of the applications
- Develop the Angular applications

Senior Software Developer - Java/Angular

2017 - 2019

Work for the company siParadigm:

- Develop the backend system using Java
- Develop the customer portal with Angular
- Optimize the complex SQL queries
- Create PDF and Word reports

Projects

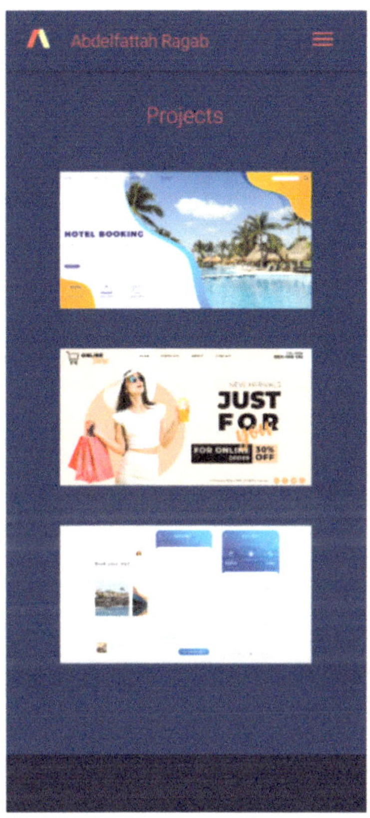

Contact

Giza, Giza Governorate, Egypt

Abdelfattah Ragab

1.3 Preview (Desktop)

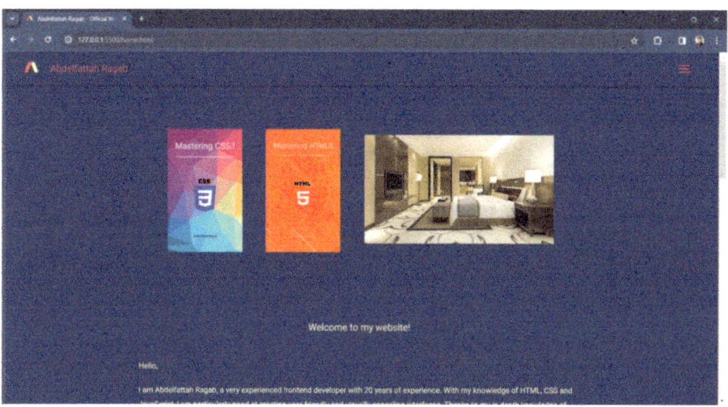

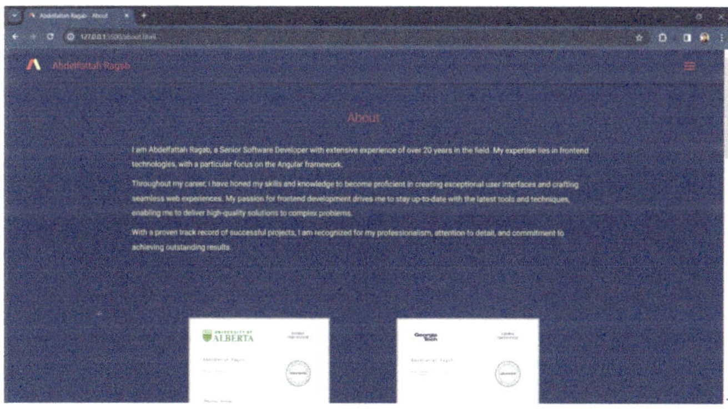

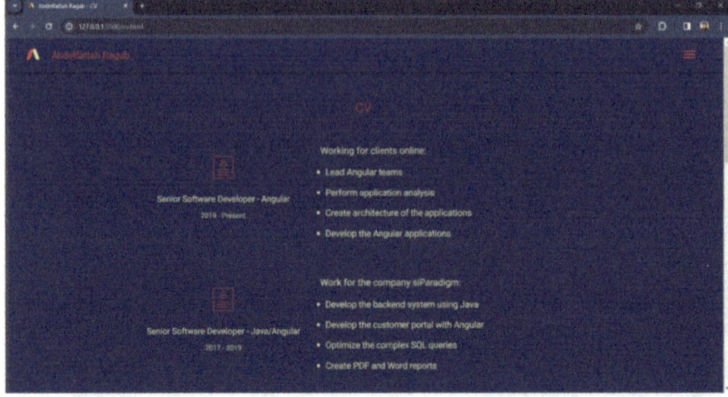
Abdelfattah Ragab
CV
Senior Software Developer - Angular
2019 - Present
Working for clients online:
Lead Angular teams
Perform application analysis
Create architecture of the applications
Develop the Angular applications
Senior Software Developer - Java/Angular
2017 - 2019
Work for the company siParadigm:
Develop the backend system using Java
Develop the customer portal with Angular
Optimize the complex SQL queries
Create PDF and Word reports

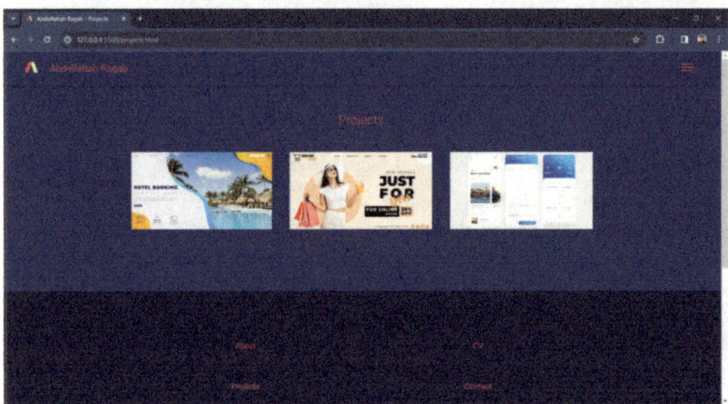
Abdelfattah Ragab
Projects
HOTEL BOOKING
JUST FOR
About
CV
Projects
Contact

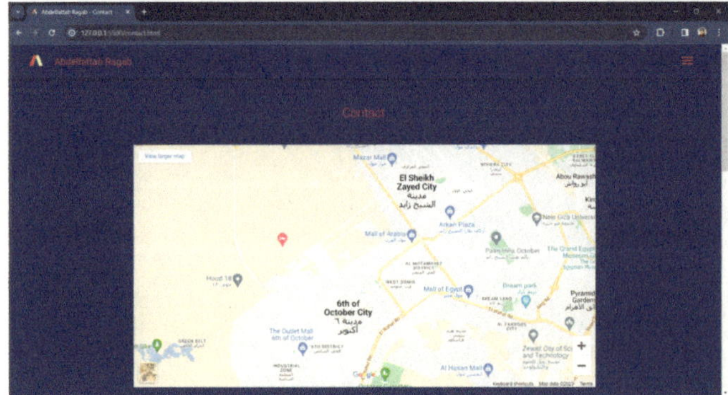
Abdelfattah Ragab
Contact
View larger map
El Sheikh Zayed City
مدينة الشيخ زايد
6th of October City
مدينة ٦ أكتوبر

1.4 Choose Colors

You can get started quickly and use the following website to help you choose colors for your website.
https://huemint.com

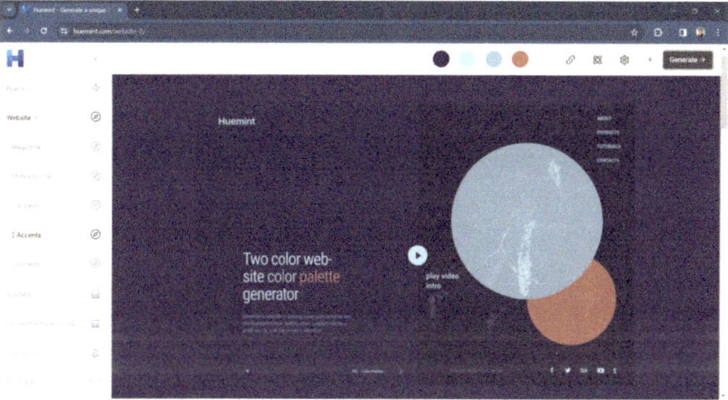

Chapter 2: App Layout

2.1 App Diagram

2.2 App Structure

```html
<app-top-bar></app-top-bar>
<app-sidenav></app-sidenav>
<main class="main">
  <router-outlet></router-outlet>
</main>
<app-footer></app-footer>
```

2.3 App Folder Structure

```
App
├── data
├── layout
│    ├── top-bar
│    ├── sidenav
│    └── footer
├── pages
│    ├── home
│    ├── about
│    ├── cv
│    ├── projects
│    └── contact
├── services
└── state
```

Chapter 3: Project Setup

3.1 Create the Angular App

```
ng new portfolio-app
```

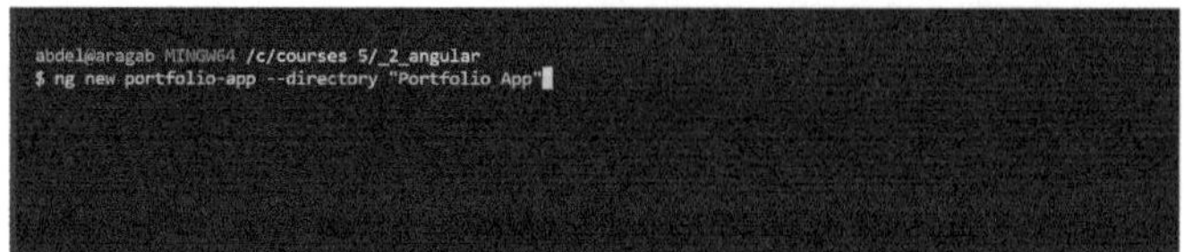

3.2 Copy the Assets

Copy the assets images and files to the "public" folder.

3.3 Set Title and Icon

In the index.html file.

Set app title

```
<title>Portfolio App</title>
```

Set app icon

```
<link rel="icon" type="image/x-icon"
href="assets/images/logo.png" />
```

```
8    <link rel="icon" type="image/x-icon" href="assets/images/logo.png" />
```

3.4 Add Global Style

Add the following to the "styles.css" file:

```css
* {
  margin: 0;
  padding: 0;
  box-sizing: border-box;
}
:root {
  --main-color: #1c4270;
  --accent-color-1: #dc5261;
  --accent-color-2: #f8f4a6;


  --footer-background: #0a2444;
  --footer-text: rgba(248, 244, 166, 0.7);
}
html,
body {
  font-family: Roboto, Arial, Helvetica,
sans-serif;
  color: var(--accent-color-2);
  background-color: var(--accent-color-1);
  line-height: 1.5rem !important;
  min-height: 100%;
```

```css
    position: relative;
    overflow-x: hidden;
}
body {
  background-color: var(--main-color);
}
.link {
  cursor: pointer;
  color: var(--accent-color-1);
  text-decoration: none;
}
a:link,
a:visited,
.link:link,
.link:visited {
  color: var(--accent-color-1);
  text-decoration: none;
}
.link:hover,
a:hover {
  filter: brightness(1.1);
}
.main {
  margin: auto;
  padding: 100px 40px;
  @media (min-width: 760px) {
```

```css
    width: 70%;
    padding: 120px 40px;
  }
}
.main-title {
  font-size: 26px;
  font-weight: 300;
  text-align: center;
  color: var(--accent-color-1);
  padding-top: 10px;
  padding-bottom: 30px;
}
```

3.5 Clean the app.component.html

Remove everything from the "app.component.html" file except the `router-outlet`

Wrap it within the main element as follows

```html
<main class="main">
  <router-outlet></router-outlet>
</main>
```

Chapter 4: Top Bar Component

4.1 Preview

4.2 Create It

```
ng g c layout/top-bar
```

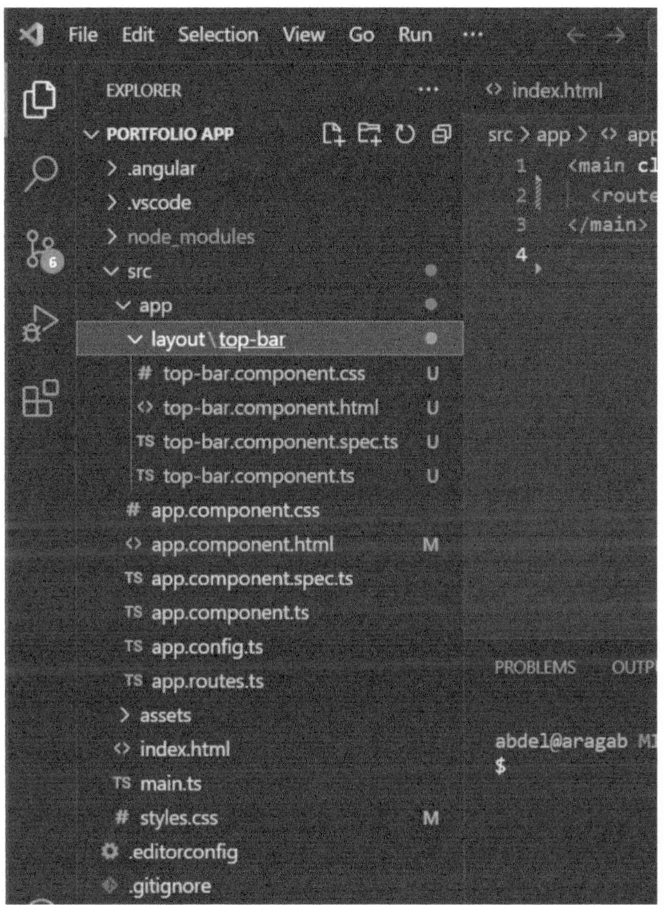

4.3 HTML

Paste this HTML code into top-bar.component.html

```html
<header class="top-bar">
  <div class="brand">
```

```html
    <img routerLink="/"
src="assets/images/logo.png" alt="" class="logo
link" />
    <div class="brand-name link"
routerLink="/">Abdelfattah Ragab</div>
  </div>
  <div class="menu-button">
    <img src="assets/images/other/menu.png"
alt="" class="menu-icon link" />
  </div>
</header>
```

```html
1   <header class="top-bar">
2     <div class="brand">
3       <img routerLink="/" src="assets/images/logo.png" alt="" class="logo link" />
4       <div class="brand-name link" routerLink="/">Abdelfattah Ragab</div>
5     </div>
6     <div class="menu-button">
7       <img src="assets/images/other/menu.png" alt="" class="menu-icon link" />
8     </div>
9   </header>
10
```

4.4 CSS

Paste this CSS code into the top-bar.component.css

```css
.top-bar {
  display: flex;
  width: 100%;
  height: 70px;
  justify-content: space-between;
  align-items: center;
  padding: 10px 20px;
  background-color: var(--main-color);
  color: var(--accent-color-1);
  box-shadow: 0 2px 5px #0000004d;
  position: fixed;
  z-index: 5;
  font-size: 26px;
```

```css
  @media (min-width: 760px) {
    padding: 10px 40px;
  }
}
.brand {
  display: flex;
  flex-direction: row;
  justify-content: flex-start;
  align-items: center;
  cursor: pointer;
  gap: 20px;
}
.brand-name {
  font-size: 20px;
  padding: 20px 0px;
}
.logo {
  width: 39px;
  height: auto;
  display: flex;
  justify-content: center;
  align-items: center;
}
.menu-icon {
  width: 50px;
  padding: 12px;
}
```

4.5 Use It

Import it into the app.component.ts

```typescript
import { Component } from '@angular/core';
import { CommonModule } from '@angular/common';
```

```typescript
import { RouterOutlet } from '@angular/router';
import { TopBarComponent } from
'./layout/top-bar/top-bar.component';

@Component({
  selector: 'app-root',
  standalone: true,
  imports: [CommonModule, RouterOutlet,
TopBarComponent],
  templateUrl: './app.component.html',
  styleUrl: './app.component.css',
})
export class AppComponent {
  title = 'portfolio-app';
}
```

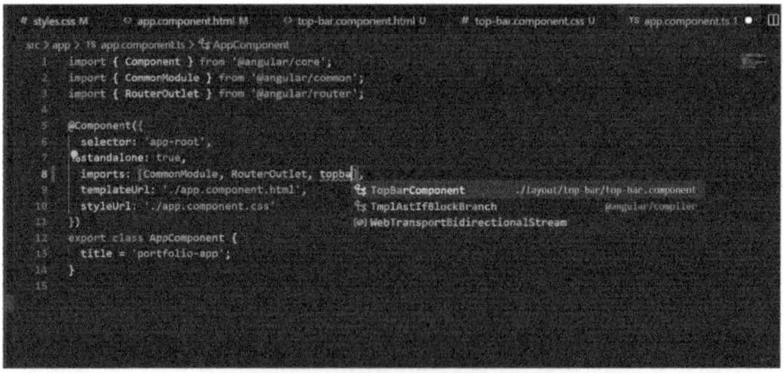

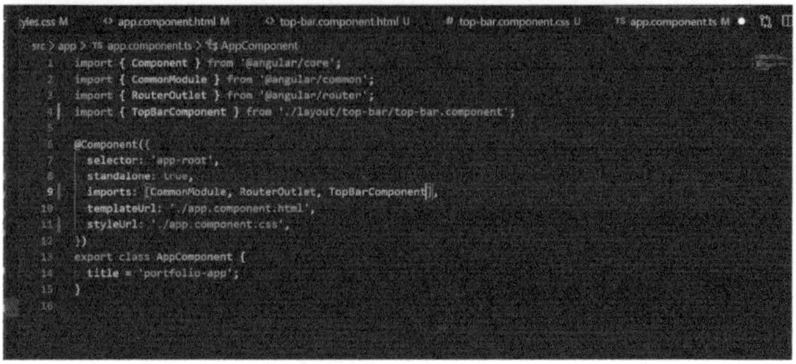

Use it in the app.component.html before the `router-outlet`

```
<app-top-bar></app-top-bar>
```

```
tyles.css M      <> app.component.html M ●      <> top-bar.component.html U      # top-bar.component.css U      TS app.com
src > app > <> app.component.html > ⊘ app-top-bar
1   <app-top-bar></app-top-bar>
2   <main class="main">
3     <router-outlet></router-outlet>
4   </main>
5
```

Chapter 5: Sidenav State

5.1 Sidenav Service

5.1.1 Create It

```
ng g s services/sidenav
```

```
abdel@aragab MINGW64 ~/Documents/temp/Portfolio App (master)
$ ng g s services/sidenav
```

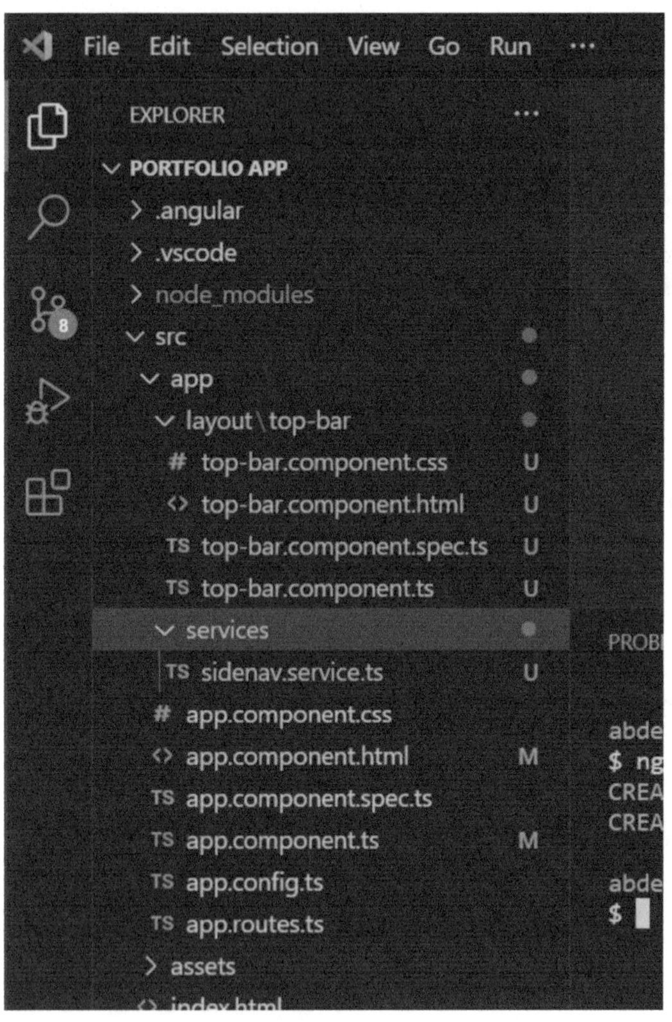

I have deleted the spec file

5.1.2 TS

Here is the TypeScript code for the Service

```typescript
import { Injectable } from '@angular/core';

@Injectable({
  providedIn: 'root',
})
export class SidenavService {
  getItems() {
    return [
      { title: 'Home', path: 'home' },
      { title: 'About', path: 'about' },
      { title: 'CV', path: 'cv' },
      { title: 'Projects', path: 'projects' },
      { title: 'Contact', path: 'contact' },
    ];
  }
}
```

5.2 Sidenav State

5.2.1 Create It

Create a "state" folder in the "app" folder.
Create a "sidenav.store.ts" file in the "state" folder.

```typescript
import { patchState, signalStore, withMethods,
withState } from '@ngrx/signals';
import { inject } from '@angular/core';
import { SidenavService } from
'../services/sidenav.service';

type SidenavState = {
  items: any[];
  isOpen: boolean;
};
```

```typescript
const initialState: SidenavState = {
  items: [],
  isOpen: false,
};

export const SidenavStore = signalStore(
  { providedIn: 'root' },
  withState(initialState),
  withMethods((store, sidenavService =
inject(SidenavService)) => ({
    loadItems: async () => {
      const items: any =
sidenavService.getItems();
      patchState(store, (state) => ({
        ...state,
        items,
      }));
    },
    open: () => {
      patchState(store, (state) => ({ ...state,
isOpen: true }));
    },
    close: () => {
      patchState(store, (state) => ({ ...state,
isOpen: false }));
    },
    toggle: () => {
      patchState(store, (state) => ({ ...state,
isOpen: !store.isOpen() }));
    },
  }))
);
```

Chapter 6: Sidenav Component

6.1 Preview

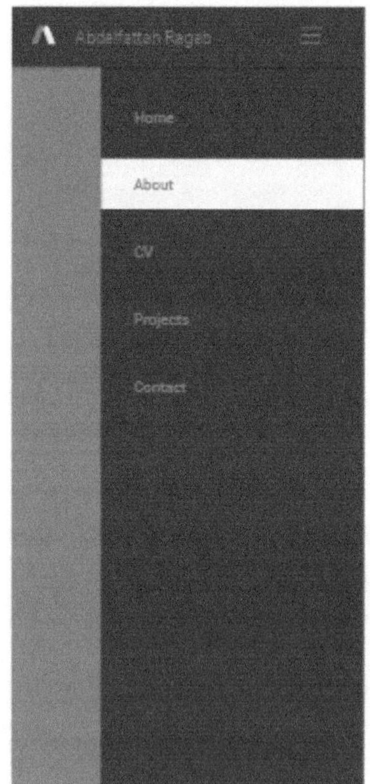

6.2 Create It

```
ng g c layout/sidenav
```

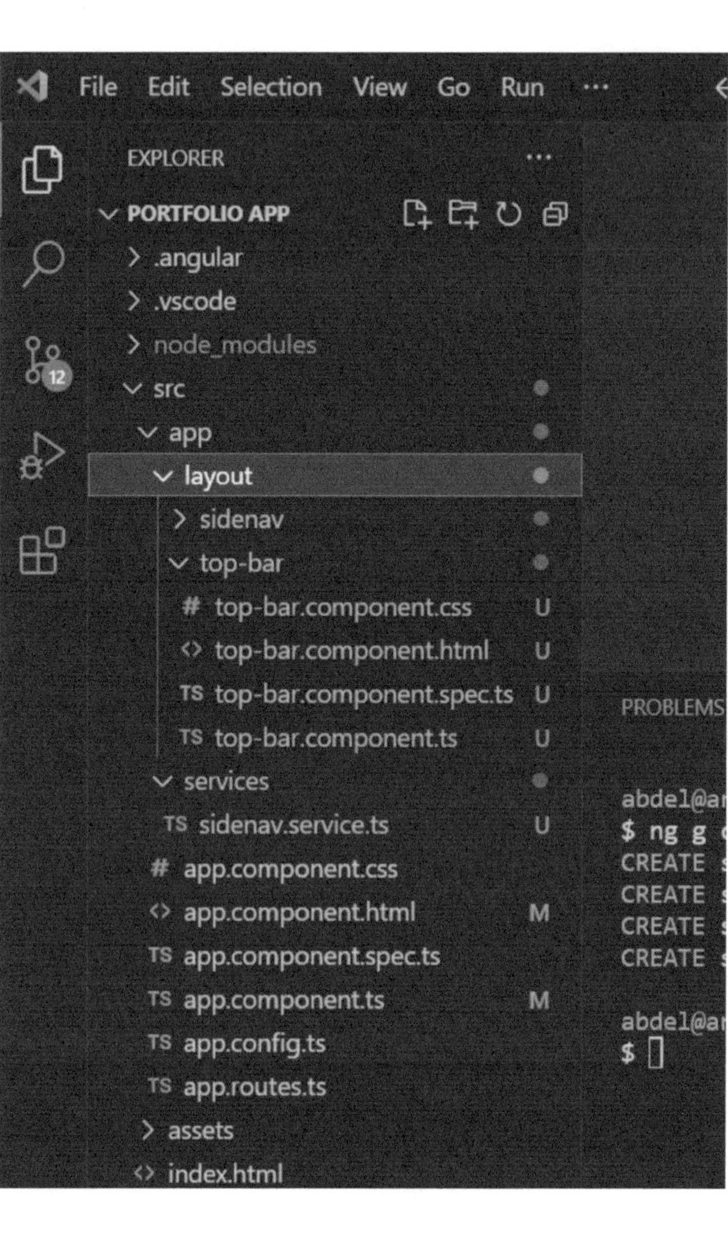

File   Edit   Selection   View   Go   Run   ...
EXPLORER
PORTFOLIO APP
.angular
.vscode
node_modules
src
app
layout
sidenav
top-bar
top-bar.component.css   U
top-bar.component.html   U
top-bar.component.spec.ts   U
top-bar.component.ts   U
services
sidenav.service.ts   U
app.component.css
app.component.html   M
app.component.spec.ts
app.component.ts   M
app.config.ts
app.routes.ts
assets
index.html
PROBLEMS
abdel@ar
$ ng g
CREATE
CREATE
CREATE
CREATE
abdel@ar
$

6.3 TS

Here is the TypeScript code of the component

```typescript
import { CommonModule } from '@angular/common';
import {
  Component,
  EventEmitter,
  inject,
  Input,
  OnInit,
  Output,
} from '@angular/core';
import { SidenavStore } from
'../../state/sidenav.store';
import { Router } from '@angular/router';

@Component({
  selector: 'app-sidenav',
  imports: [CommonModule],
  templateUrl: './sidenav.component.html',
  styleUrl: './sidenav.component.css',
})
export class SidenavComponent implements OnInit
{
  sidenavStore = inject(SidenavStore);
  router = inject(Router);

  onItemClicked(itemName: string) {
    this.router.navigate(['/', itemName]);
    this.sidenavStore.close();
  }

  ngOnInit(): void {
    this.sidenavStore.loadItems();
```

```
    }
}
```

6.4 HTML

Here is the HTML code for the component

```html
<div
  class="backdrop"
  [ngClass]="{ 'backdrop-visible':
sidenavStore.isOpen() }"
></div>
<nav class="sidenav" [ngClass]="{
'sidenav-visible': sidenavStore.isOpen() }">
  @for(sidenavItem of sidenavStore.items();
track sidenavItem.title) {
  <div
(click)="onItemClicked(sidenavItem.path)"
class="sidenav-item">
    {{ sidenavItem.title }}
  </div>
  }
</nav>
```

6.5 CSS

```css
.backdrop {
  width: 100vw;
  height: 100vh;
  background-color: rgba(0, 0, 0, 0.6);
  position: fixed;
  top: 0;
  left: 0;
```

```css
    z-index: 3;
    display: none;
}
.backdrop-visible {
    display: block;
}
.sidenav {
    width: 320px;
    height: 100%;
    min-height: 100vh;
    box-shadow: 1px 1px 3px 1px gray;
    background-color: var(--main-color);
    display: flex !important;
    flex-direction: column;
    gap: 20px;
    padding-top: 100px;
    position: absolute;
    top: 0px;
    right: -320px;
    transition: all 300ms;
    z-index: 4;
    overflow: hidden;
}
.sidenav-visible {
    right: 0px;
}
.sidenav-item {
    padding: 0px 40px;
    width: 100%;
    height: 60px;
    text-decoration: none;
    display: flex;
    justify-content: flex-start;
    align-items: center;
```

```css
    font-size: 18px;
    font-weight: 500;
    color: var(--accent-color-1);
    cursor: pointer;
}
.sidenav-item:hover {
    background-color: var(--accent-color-2);
}
```

6.6 Use It

Update the app.component.ts to the following

```typescript
import { CommonModule } from '@angular/common';
import { Component } from '@angular/core';
import { RouterOutlet } from '@angular/router';
import { SidenavComponent } from
'./layout/sidenav/sidenav.component';
import { TopBarComponent } from
'./layout/top-bar/top-bar.component';

@Component({
  selector: 'app-root',
  imports: [
    CommonModule,
    RouterOutlet,
    TopBarComponent,
    SidenavComponent
  ],
  templateUrl: './app.component.html',
  styleUrl: './app.component.css',
})
export class AppComponent {}
```

Use it in the app.component.html as follows

```
<app-top-bar></app-top-bar>
<app-sidenav></app-sidenav>
<main class="main">
  <router-outlet></router-outlet>
</main>
```

6.7 Update top-bar Component

```
import { CommonModule } from '@angular/common';
import { Component, inject } from
'@angular/core';
import { RouterModule } from '@angular/router';
import { SidenavStore } from
'../../state/sidenav.store';

@Component({
  selector: 'app-top-bar',
  imports: [CommonModule, RouterModule],
  templateUrl: './top-bar.component.html',
  styleUrl: './top-bar.component.css',
})
export class TopBarComponent {
  sidenavStore = inject(SidenavStore);
}
```

Update the HTML

```
<header class="top-bar">
  <div class="brand">
    <img routerLink="/"
src="assets/images/logo.png" alt="" class="logo
link" />
```

```html
    <div class="brand-name link"
routerLink="/">Abdelfattah Ragab</div>
  </div>
  <div class="menu-button">
    <img
      src="assets/images/other/menu.png"
      (click)="sidenavStore.toggle()"
      alt=""
      class="menu-icon link"
    />
  </div>
</header>
```

Chapter 7: Footer Component

7.1 Preview

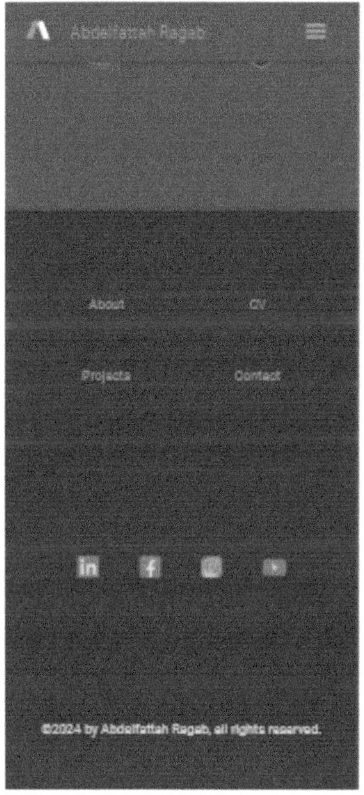

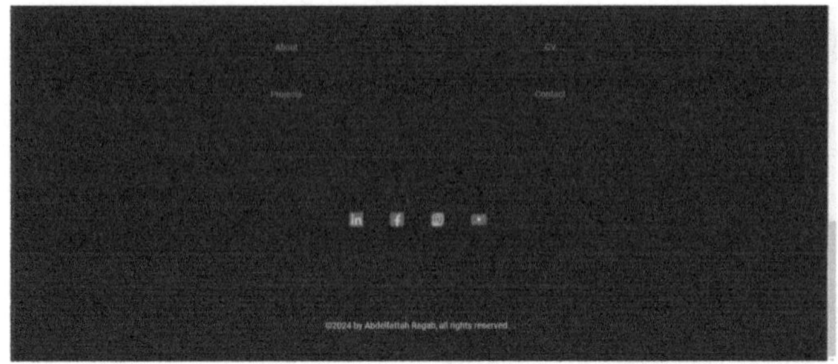

7.2 Create It

```
ng g c layout/footer
```

```
abdel@aragab MINGW64 ~/Documents/temp/Portfolio App (master)
$ ng g c layout/footer
```

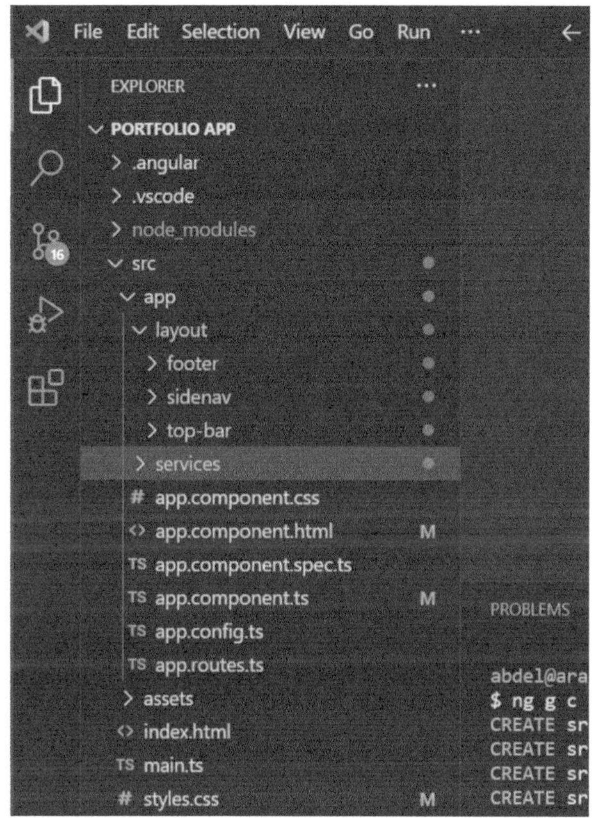

7.3 TS

No changes

7.4 HTML

```html
<footer class="footer">
```

```html
<section class="main-footer">
  <div routerLink="/about"
class="link">About</div>
  <div routerLink="/cv" class="link">CV</div>
  <div routerLink="/projects"
class="link">Projects</div>
  <div routerLink="/contact"
class="link">Contact</div>
</section>
<div class="divider"></div>
<section class="social-footer">
  <a href=""
    ><img
src="assets/images/social/linkedin.png" alt=""
class="social-icon"
  /></a>
  <a href=""
    ><img
src="assets/images/social/facebook.png" alt=""
class="social-icon"
  /></a>
  <a href=""
    ><img
src="assets/images/social/instagram.png" alt=""
class="social-icon"
  /></a>
  <a href=""
    ><img
      src="assets/images/social/youtube.png"
      alt=""
      class="social-icon youtube-icon"
  /></a>
</section>
<div class="divider"></div>
```

```html
<section class="copyright-footer">
  <p>©2024 by Abdelfattah Ragab, all rights reserved.</p>
</section>
</footer>
```

7.5 CSS

```css
.footer {
  background-color: var(--footer-background);
}
.main-footer {
  padding: 100px 60px;
  display: grid;
  grid-template-columns: 1fr 1fr;
  place-items: center center;
  gap: 60px;
  @media (min-width: 760px) {
    padding: 100px 300px;
  }
}
.divider {
  width: 70%;
  height: 1px;
  margin: auto;
  background-color: var(--accent-color-2);
  opacity: 0.1;
  @media (min-width: 760px) {
    width: 40%;
  }
}
.social-footer {
  display: flex;
```

```css
  gap: 50px;
  justify-content: center;
  padding: 100px 60px;
  align-items: center;
  background-color: var(--footer-background);
}
.social-footer .social-icon {
  width: 26px;
  height: auto;
  opacity: 0.8;
}
.youtube-icon {
  transform: scale(1.12);
}
.copyright-footer {
  display: flex;
  justify-content: center;
  align-items: center;
  background-color: var(--footer-background);
  color: var(--footer-text);
  padding: 60px 0;
  cursor: default;
}
```

7.6 Use It

Import it into the app.component.ts as follows

```typescript
import { FooterComponent } from
'./layout/footer/footer.component';

@Component({
  selector: 'app-root',
  standalone: true,
```

```typescript
  imports: [
    CommonModule,
    RouterOutlet,
    TopBarComponent,
    SidenavComponent,
    FooterComponent,
  ],
  templateUrl: './app.component.html',
  styleUrl: './app.component.css',
})
export class AppComponent implements OnInit {
```

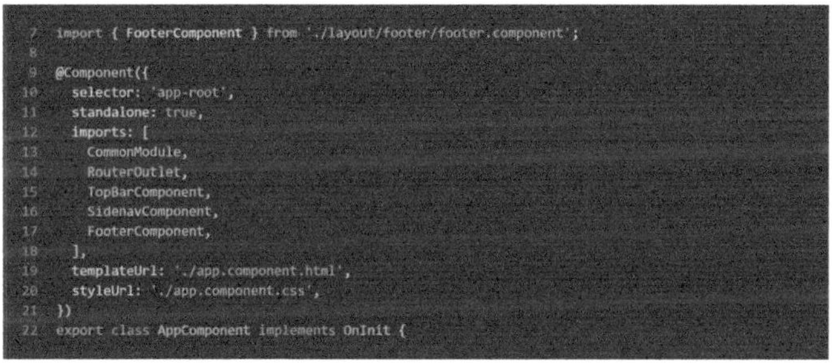

```typescript
7   import { FooterComponent } from './layout/footer/footer.component';
8
9   @Component({
10    selector: 'app-root',
11    standalone: true,
12    imports: [
13      CommonModule,
14      RouterOutlet,
15      TopBarComponent,
16      SidenavComponent,
17      FooterComponent,
18    ],
19    templateUrl: './app.component.html',
20    styleUrl: './app.component.css',
21  })
22  export class AppComponent implements OnInit {
```

Use it in the app.component.html as follows

```html
...
  <router-outlet></router-outlet>
</main>
<app-footer></app-footer>
```

```html
7     <router-outlet></router-outlet>
8   </main>
9   <app-footer></app-footer>
```

Chapter 8: Home Page

8.1 Preview

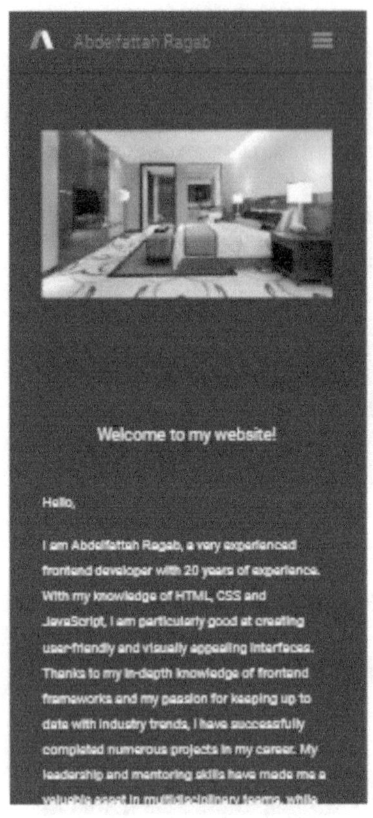

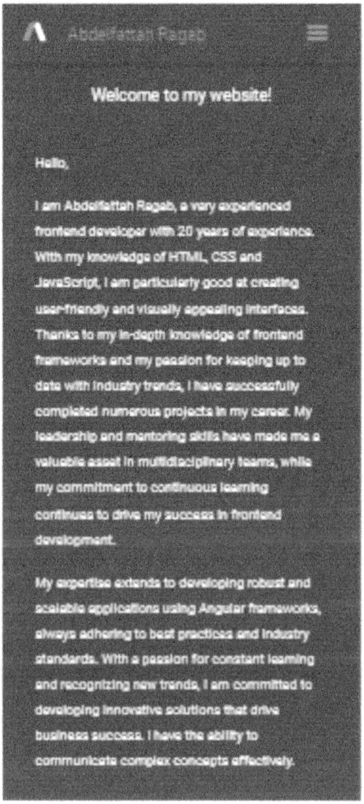

Welcome to my website!

Hello,

I am Abdelfattah Ragab, a very experienced frontend developer with 20 years of experience. With my knowledge of HTML, CSS and JavaScript, I am particularly good at creating user-friendly and visually appealing interfaces. Thanks to my in-depth knowledge of frontend frameworks and my passion for keeping up to date with industry trends, I have successfully completed numerous projects in my career. My leadership and mentoring skills have made me a valuable asset in multidisciplinary teams, while my commitment to continuous learning continues to drive my success in frontend development.

My expertise extends to developing robust and scalable applications using Angular frameworks, always adhering to best practices and industry standards. With a passion for constant learning and recognizing new trends, I am committed to developing innovative solutions that drive business success. I have the ability to communicate complex concepts effectively.

My expertise extends to developing robust and scalable applications using Angular frameworks, always adhering to best practices and industry standards. With a passion for constant learning and recognizing new trends, I am committed to developing innovative solutions that drive business success. I have the ability to communicate complex concepts effectively.

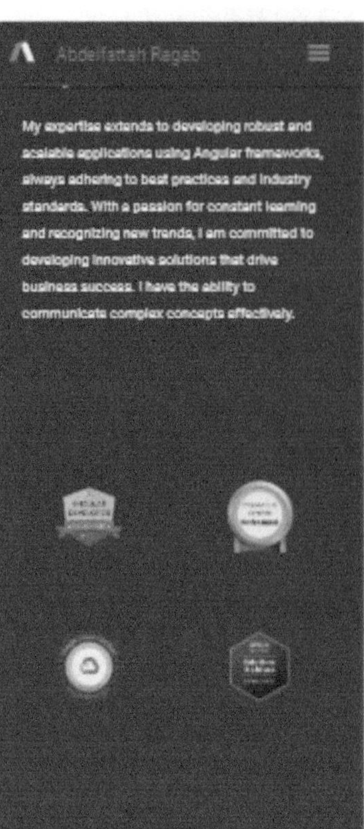

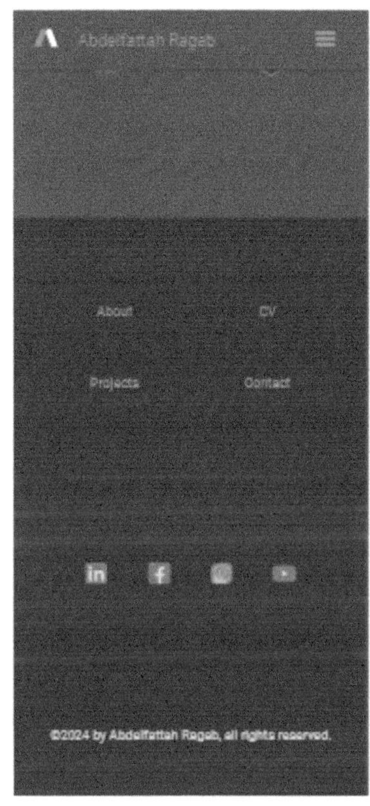
Abdelfattah Ragab
About
CV
Projects
Contact
©2024 by Abdelfattah Ragab, all rights reserved.

Abdelfattah Ragab - Official Si
Abdelfattah Ragab
Mastering CSS3
Mastering HTML5
CSS
HTML
Welcome to my website!
Hello,
I am Abdelfattah Ragab, a very experienced frontend developer with 20 years of experience. With my knowledge of HTML, CSS and

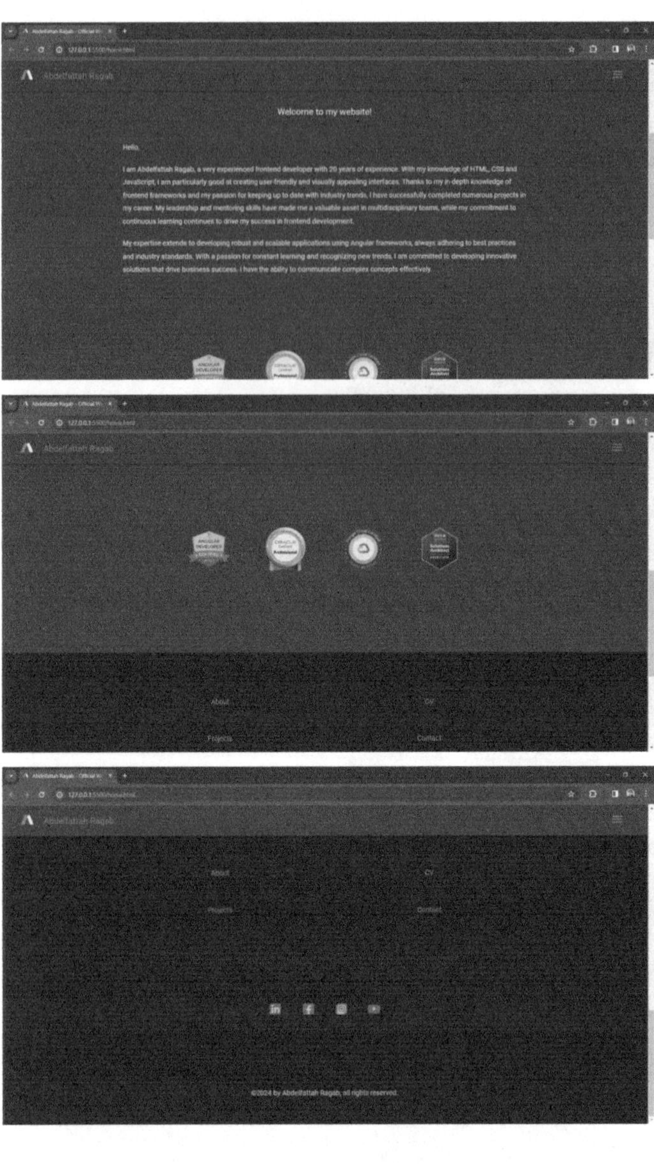
Abdelfattah Ragab
Welcome to my website!
Hello,
I am Abdelfattah Ragab, a very experienced frontend developer with 20 years of experience. With my knowledge of HTML, CSS and JavaScript, I am particularly good at creating user-friendly and visually appealing interfaces. Thanks to my in-depth knowledge of frontend frameworks and my passion for keeping up to date with industry trends, I have successfully completed numerous projects in my career. My leadership and mentoring skills have made me a valuable asset in multidisciplinary teams, while my commitment to continuous learning continues to drive my success in frontend development.
My expertise extends to developing robust and scalable applications using Angular frameworks, always adhering to best practices and industry standards. With a passion for constant learning and recognizing new trends, I am committed to developing innovative solutions that drive business success. I have the ability to communicate complex concepts effectively.
About
CV
Projects
Contact
©2024 by Abdelfattah Ragab, all rights reserved.

8.2 Page Outline

```
<app-promotion></app-promotion>
<app-welcome></app-welcome>
<app-badges></app-badges>
```

8.3 Create It

```
ng g c pages/home
```

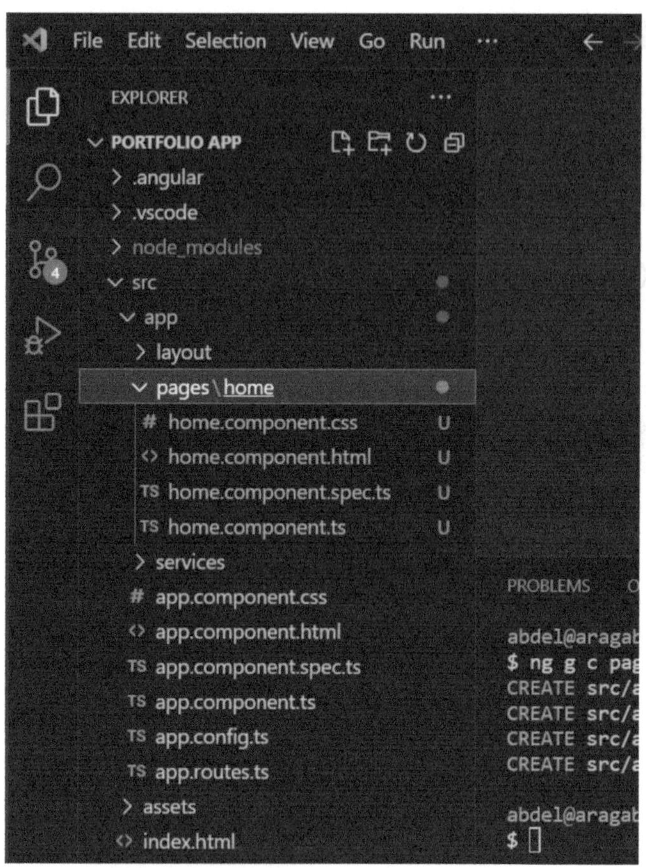

8.4 Add Route

Update app.route.ts as follows

```
import { Routes } from '@angular/router';
import { HomeComponent } from
'./pages/home/home.component';
```

```typescript
export const routes: Routes = [
  { path: '', redirectTo: 'home', pathMatch: 'full' },
  { path: 'home', component: HomeComponent },
];
```

```
1  import { Routes } from '@angular/router';
2  import { HomeComponent } from './pages/home/home.component';
3
4  export const routes: Routes = [
5    { path: '', redirectTo: 'home', pathMatch: 'full' },
6    { path: 'home', component: HomeComponent },
7  ];
8
```

Chapter 9: [Home] Promotion Component

9.1 Preview

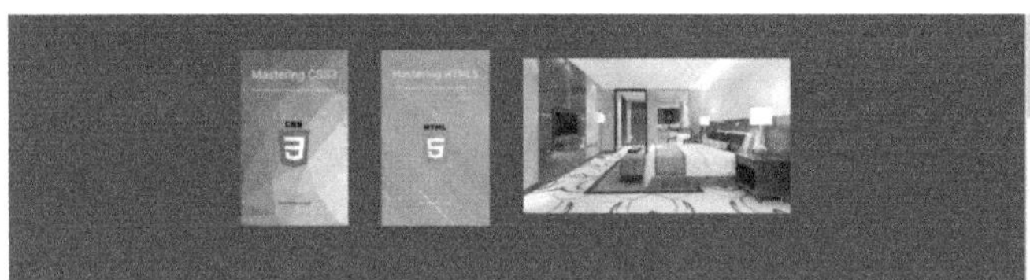

9.2 Create It

```
ng g c pages/home/components/promotion
```

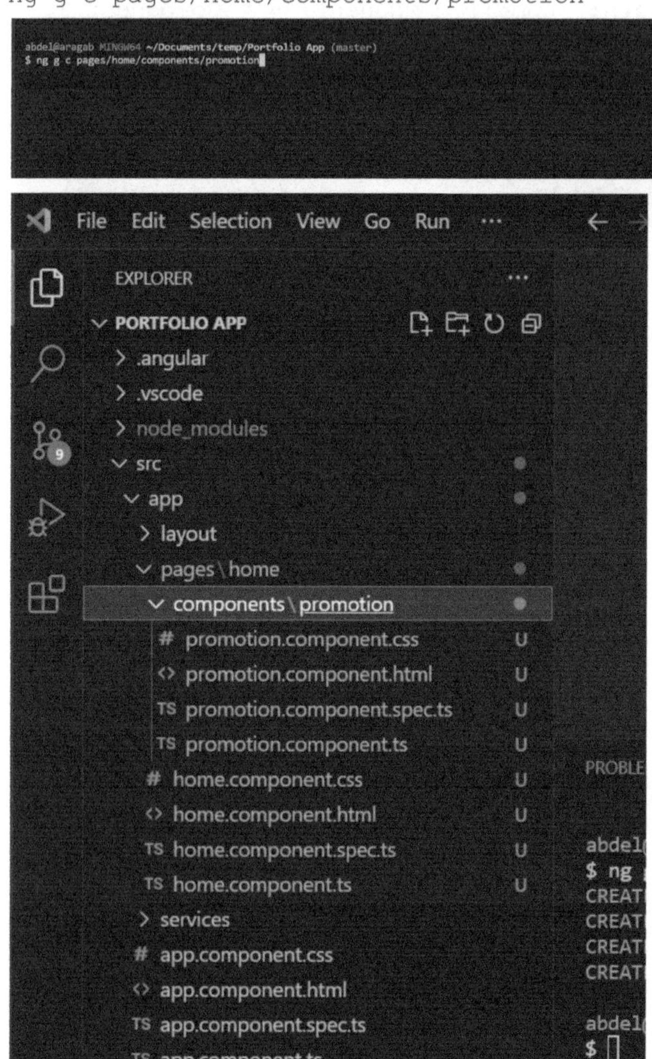

9.3 TS

No changes

9.4 HTML

```html
<section class="promotion">
  <img

src="assets/images/promotion/book-mastering-css
3.jpg"
    alt=""
    title="Mastering CSS3 A Comprehensive Guide
to Modern Web Styling"
    class="book link"
  />
  <img

src="assets/images/promotion/book-mastering-htm
l5.jpg"
    alt=""
    title="Mastering HTML5: The Complete Guide
to Modern Web Development"
    class="book link"
  />
  <img

src="assets/images/promotion/course-hotel-booki
ng-app.jpg"
    alt=""
    title="Creative CSS Projects: Hotel Booking
App"
    class="course link"
```

```
  />
</section>
```

```
1   <section class="promotion">
2     <img
3       src="assets/images/promotion/book-mastering-css3.jpg"
4       alt=""
5       title="Mastering CSS3 A Comprehensive Guide to Modern Web Styling"
6       class="book link"
7     />
8     <img
9       src="assets/images/promotion/book-mastering-html5.jpg"
10      alt=""
11      title="Mastering HTML5: The Complete Guide to Modern Web Development"
12      class="book link"
13    />
14    <img
15      src="assets/images/promotion/course-hotel-booking-app.jpg"
16      alt=""
17      title="Creative CSS Projects: Hotel Booking App"
18      class="course link"
19    />
20  </section>
21
```

9.5 CSS

```css
.promotion {
  display: flex;
  justify-content: center;
  align-items: center;
  padding: 40px 20px;
  @media (min-width: 760px) {
    gap: 50px;
    padding: 40px 20px;
  }
}
.book {
  width: 160px;
  height: auto;
  max-height: 100%;
  cursor: pointer;
  display: none;
  @media (min-width: 760px) {
    display: block;
```

```scss
    }
  }
  .course {
    max-width: 100%;
    height: auto;
    max-height: 100%;
    cursor: pointer;
    @media (min-width: 760px) {
      width: 400px;
    }
  }
}
```

```scss
 1  .promotion {
 2    display: flex;
 3    justify-content: center;
 4    align-items: center;
 5    padding: 40px 20px;
 6    @media (min-width: 760px) {
 7      gap: 50px;
 8      padding: 40px 20px;
 9    }
10  }
11  .book {
12    width: 160px;
13    height: auto;
14    max-height: 100%;
15    cursor: pointer;
16    display: none;
17    @media (min-width: 760px) {
18      display: block;
19    }
20  }
21  .course {
22    max-width: 100%;
23    height: auto;
24    max-height: 100%;
25    cursor: pointer;
26    @media (min-width: 760px) {
27      width: 400px;
28    }
29  }
30
```

9.6 Use It

Import it into home.component.ts

```typescript
import { Component } from '@angular/core';
```

```typescript
import { PromotionComponent } from
'./components/promotion/promotion.component';

@Component({
  selector: 'app-home',
  standalone: true,
  imports: [PromotionComponent],
  templateUrl: './home.component.html',
  styleUrl: './home.component.css',
})
export class HomeComponent {}
```

```typescript
1   import { Component } from '@angular/core';
2   import { PromotionComponent } from './components/promotion/promotion.component';
3
4   @Component({
5     selector: 'app-home',
6     standalone: true,
7     imports: [PromotionComponent],
8     templateUrl: './home.component.html',
9     styleUrl: './home.component.css',
10  })
11  export class HomeComponent {}
12
```

Use it in the home.component.html

```html
<app-promotion></app-promotion>
```

```html
1   <app-promotion></app-promotion>
```

Chapter 10: [Home] Welcome Component

10.1 Preview

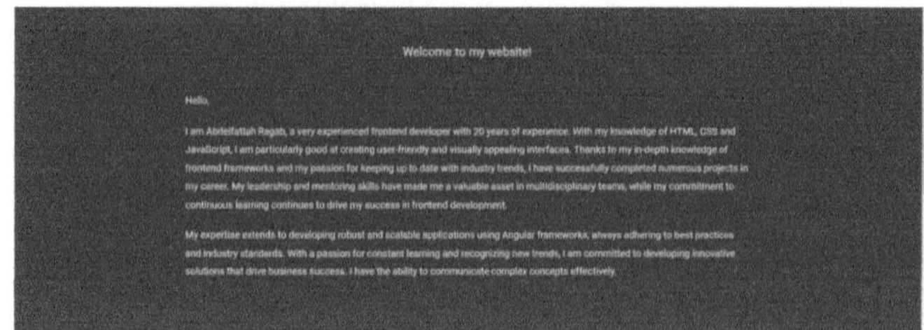

10.2 Create It

```
ng g c pages/home/components/welcome
```

```
abdel@aragab MINGW64 ~/Documents/temp/Portfolio App (master)
$ ng g c pages/home/components/welcome
```

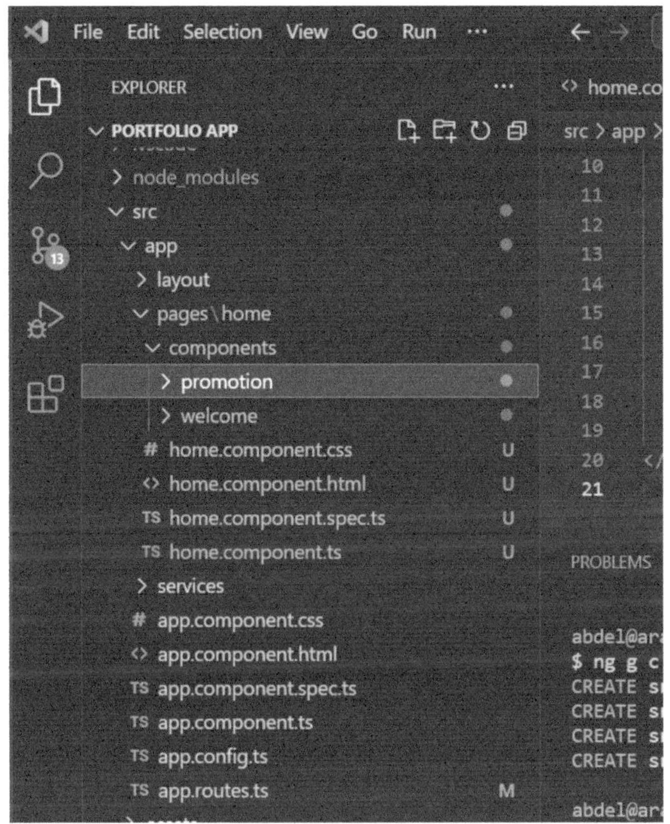

10.3 TS

No changes

10.4 HTML

```
<section class="welcome">
```

```html
<header class="welcome-header">Welcome to my
website!</header>
  <div class="welcome-content">
    <p>Hello,</p>
    <p>
      I am Abdelfattah Ragab, a very
experienced frontend developer with 20
      years of experience. With my knowledge of
HTML, CSS and JavaScript, I am
      particularly good at creating
user-friendly and visually appealing
      interfaces. Thanks to my in-depth
knowledge of frontend frameworks and my
      passion for keeping up to date with
industry trends, I have successfully
      completed numerous projects in my career.
My leadership and mentoring
      skills have made me a valuable asset in
multidisciplinary teams, while my
      commitment to continuous learning
continues to drive my success in
      frontend development.
    </p>
    <p>
      My expertise extends to developing robust
and scalable applications using
      Angular frameworks, always adhering to
best practices and industry
      standards. With a passion for constant
learning and recognizing new
      trends, I am committed to developing
innovative solutions that drive
      business success. I have the ability to
communicate complex concepts
```

```
      effectively.
    </p>
  </div>
</section>
```

10.5 CSS

```css
.welcome {
  padding: 100px 20px;
  line-height: 30px;
  cursor: default;
}
.welcome-header {
  text-align: center;
  font-size: 20px;
  margin-bottom: 40px;
}
.welcome-content p {
  padding: 10px 0px;
}
```

10.6 Use It

Import it in home.component.ts

```typescript
import { Component } from '@angular/core';
import { PromotionComponent } from
'./components/promotion/promotion.component';
import { WelcomeComponent } from
'./components/welcome/welcome.component';
```

```typescript
@Component({
  selector: 'app-home',
  standalone: true,
  imports: [PromotionComponent,
WelcomeComponent],
  templateUrl: './home.component.html',
  styleUrl: './home.component.css',
})
export class HomeComponent {}
```

```typescript
1   import { Component } from '@angular/core';
2   import { PromotionComponent } from './components/promotion/promotion.component';
3   import { WelcomeComponent } from './components/welcome/welcome.component';
4
5   @Component({
6     selector: 'app-home',
7     standalone: true,
8     imports: [PromotionComponent, WelcomeComponent],
9     templateUrl: './home.component.html',
10    styleUrl: './home.component.css',
11  })
12  export class HomeComponent {}
```

Use it in the home.component.html as follows

```html
<app-promotion></app-promotion>
<app-welcome></app-welcome>
```

```html
1   <app-promotion></app-promotion>
2   <app-welcome></app-welcome>
```

Chapter 11: [Home] Badges Component

11.1 Preview

11.2 Create It

```
ng g c pages/home/components/badges
```

11.3 TS

No changes

11.4 HTML

```html
<section class="badges">
  <img
    src="assets/images/badges/angular.png"
    alt=""
    title="Expert Angular Developer - Certified
Level 3"
    class="badge link"
  />
  <img
    src="assets/images/badges/oracle.png"
    alt=""
    title="Oracle Certified Professional: Java
SE 11 Developer"
    class="badge link"
  />
  <img
    src="assets/images/badges/google.png"
    alt=""
    title="Google Cloud Certified Professional
Cloud Architect"
    class="badge link"
  />
  <img
    src="assets/images/badges/aws.png"
    alt=""
    title="AWS Certified Solutions Architect
Associate"
```

```
    class="badge link"
  />
</section>
```

11.5 CSS

```css
.badges {
  display: grid;
  grid-template-columns: 1fr 1fr;
  place-items: center center;
  column-gap: 0px;
  row-gap: 80px;
  padding: 60px 0px;
  @media (min-width: 760px) {
    display: flex;
    justify-content: center;
    align-items: center;
    gap: 80px;
  }
}
.badges .badge {
  max-width: 80px;
  max-height: 80px;
  width: auto;
  height: auto;
  cursor: pointer;
  opacity: 0.9;
  @media (min-width: 760px) {
    max-width: 100px;
    max-height: 100px;
  }
}
```

11.6 Use It

Import it in the home.component.ts

```ts
import { Component } from '@angular/core';
import { PromotionComponent } from
'./components/promotion/promotion.component';
import { WelcomeComponent } from
'./components/welcome/welcome.component';
import { BadgesComponent } from
'./components/badges/badges.component';

@Component({
  selector: 'app-home',
  standalone: true,
  imports: [PromotionComponent,
WelcomeComponent, BadgesComponent],
  templateUrl: './home.component.html',
  styleUrl: './home.component.css',
})
export class HomeComponent {}
```



```ts
1   import { Component } from '@angular/core';
2   import { PromotionComponent } from './components/promotion/promotion.component';
3   import { WelcomeComponent } from './components/welcome/welcome.component';
4   import { BadgesComponent } from './components/badges/badges.component';
5
6   @Component({
7     selector: 'app-home',
8     standalone: true,
9     imports: [PromotionComponent, WelcomeComponent, BadgesComponent],
10    templateUrl: './home.component.html',
11    styleUrl: './home.component.css',
12  })
13  export class HomeComponent {}
14
```


Use it in the home.component.html

```html
<app-promotion></app-promotion>
<app-welcome></app-welcome>
<app-badges></app-badges>
```

Chapter 12: About Page

12.1 Preview

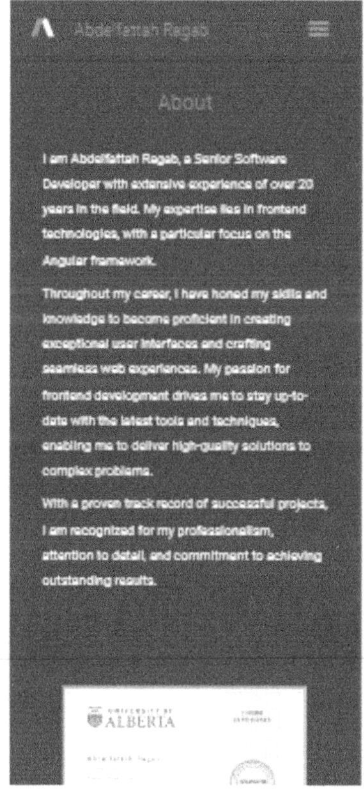

App Development with Ionic
from Scratch

AbdelFattah Ragab

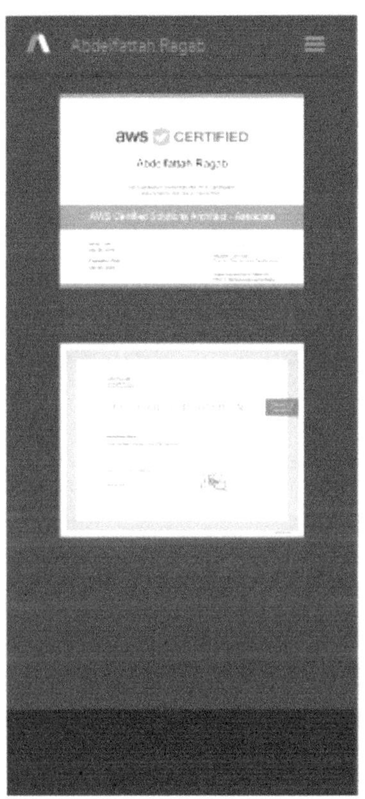

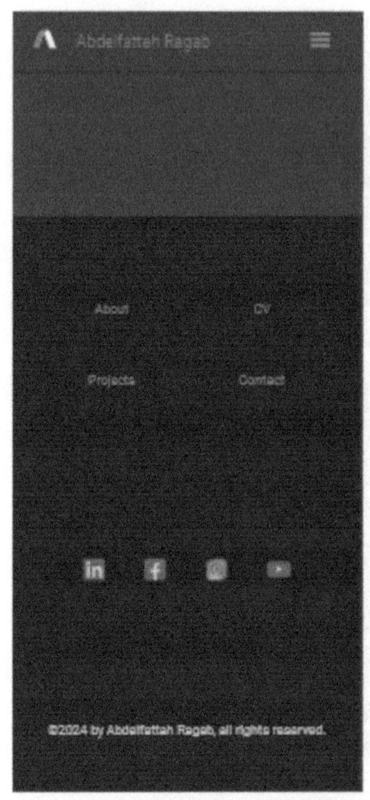
Abdelfattah Ragab
About
CV
Projects
Contact
©2024 by Abdelfattah Ragab, all rights reserved.

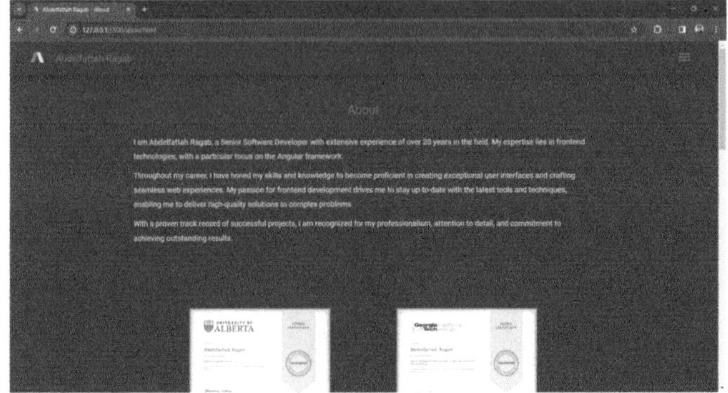
Abdelfattah Ragab - About
127.0.0.1:5500/about.html
Abdelfattah Ragab
About
I am Abdelfattah Ragab, a Senior Software Developer with extensive experience of over 20 years in the field. My expertise lies in frontend technologies, with a particular focus on the Angular framework.
Throughout my career, I have honed my skills and knowledge to become proficient in creating exceptional user interfaces and crafting seamless web experiences. My passion for frontend development drives me to stay up-to-date with the latest tools and techniques, enabling me to deliver high-quality solutions to complex problems.
With a proven track record of successful projects, I am recognized for my professionalism, attention to detail, and commitment to achieving outstanding results.
UNIVERSITY OF ALBERTA
Abdelfattah Ragab
Abdelfattah Ragab

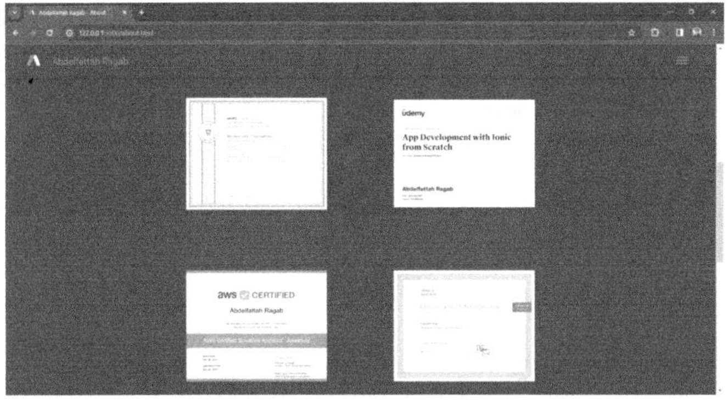

12.2 Page Outline

```
<app-bio></app-bio>
<app-certificates></app-certificates>
```

12.3 Create It

```
ng g c pages/about
```

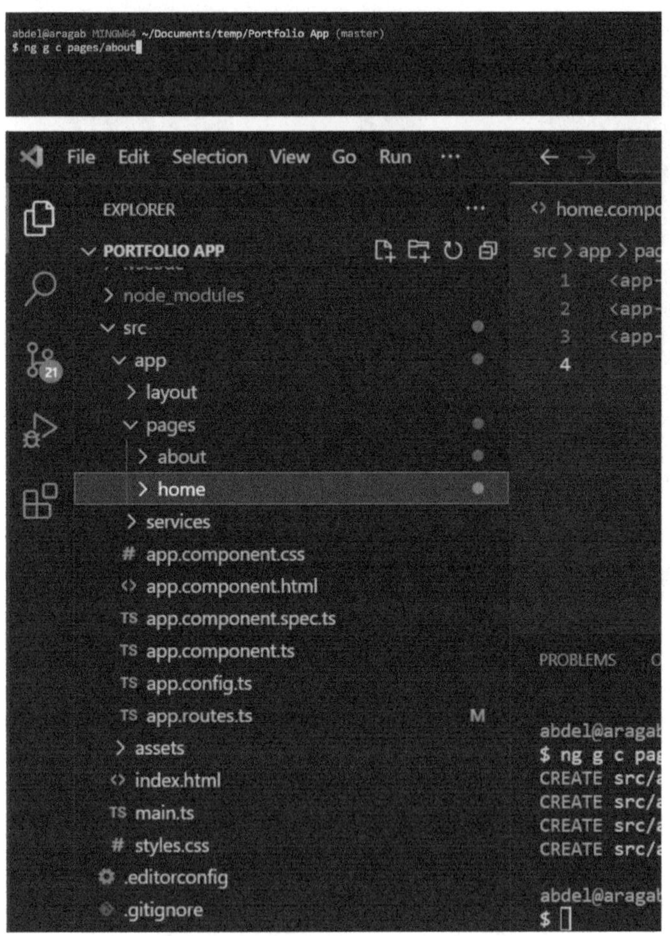

12.4 Set Title

Add title to the about.component.html

```
<header
class="main-title">About</header>
```

```
<header class="main-title">About</header>
```

12.5 Add Route

Update app.route.ts as follows

```
import { Routes } from '@angular/router';
import { HomeComponent } from
'./pages/home/home.component';
import { AboutComponent } from
'./pages/about/about.component';

export const routes: Routes = [
  { path: '', redirectTo: 'home', pathMatch:
'full' },
  { path: 'home', component: HomeComponent },
  { path: 'about', component: AboutComponent
},
];
```

```
import { Routes } from '@angular/router';
import { HomeComponent } from './pages/home/home.component';
import { AboutComponent } from './pages/about/about.component';

export const routes: Routes = [
  { path: '', redirectTo: 'home', pathMatch: 'full' },
  { path: 'home', component: HomeComponent },
  { path: 'about', component: AboutComponent },
];
```

Chapter 13: [About] Bio Component

13.1 Preview

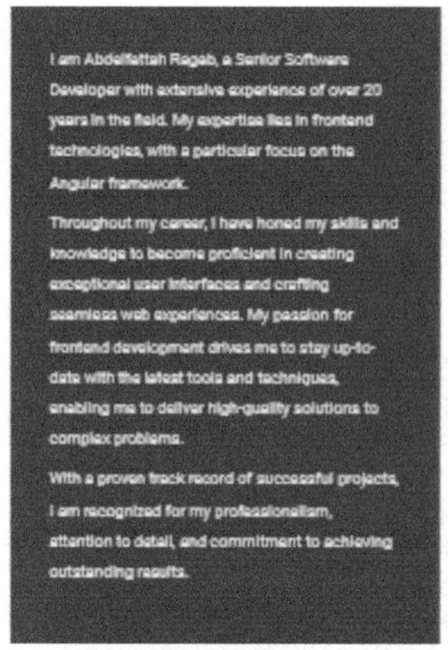

13.2 Create It

```
ng g c pages/about/components/bio
```

abdel@aragab MINGW64 ~/Documents/temp/Portfolio App (master)
$ ng g c pages/about/components/bio

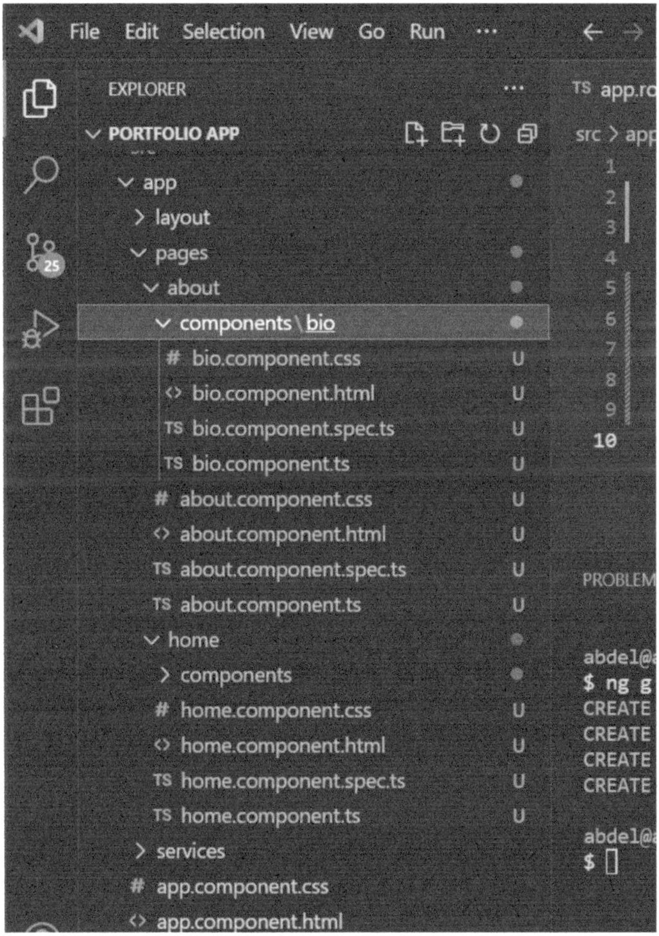

File   Edit   Selection   View   Go   Run   ...

EXPLORER
PORTFOLIO APP
app
layout
pages
about
components \ bio
bio.component.css   U
bio.component.html   U
bio.component.spec.ts   U
bio.component.ts   U
about.component.css   U
about.component.html   U
about.component.spec.ts   U
about.component.ts   U
home
components
home.component.css   U
home.component.html   U
home.component.spec.ts   U
home.component.ts   U
services
app.component.css
app.component.html

TS app.ro
src > app
1
2
3
4
5
6
7
8
9
10

PROBLEM

abdel@a
$ ng g
CREATE
CREATE
CREATE
CREATE

abdel@a
$

13.3 TS

No changes

13.4. HTML

```html
<section class="bio">
  <p>
    I am Abdelfattah Ragab, a Senior Software
Developer with extensive
    experience of over 20 years in the field.
My expertise lies in frontend
    technologies, with a particular focus on
the Angular framework.
  </p>
  <p>
    Throughout my career, I have honed my
skills and knowledge to become
    proficient in creating exceptional user
interfaces and crafting seamless web
    experiences. My passion for frontend
development drives me to stay
    up-to-date with the latest tools and
techniques, enabling me to deliver
    high-quality solutions to complex problems.
  </p>
  <p>
    With a proven track record of successful
projects, I am recognized for my
    professionalism, attention to detail, and
commitment to achieving
    outstanding results.
  </p>
```

```
</section>
```

13.5 CSS

```css
.bio p {
  margin: 10px 0px;
  line-height: 26px;
}
```

```css
1  .bio p {
2    margin: 10px 0px;
3    line-height: 26px;
4  }
```

13.6 Use It

Import it into about.component.ts

```typescript
import { Component } from '@angular/core';
import { BioComponent } from
'./components/bio/bio.component';

@Component({
  selector: 'app-about',
  standalone: true,
  imports: [BioComponent],
  templateUrl: './about.component.html',
  styleUrl: './about.component.css',
})
export class AboutComponent {}
```

```typescript
import { Component } from '@angular/core';
import { BioComponent } from './components/bio/bio.component';

@Component({
  selector: 'app-about',
  standalone: true,
  imports: [BioComponent],
  templateUrl: './about.component.html',
  styleUrl: './about.component.css',
})
export class AboutComponent {}
```

Use it in the about.component.html

```html
<header class="main-title">About</header>
<app-bio></app-bio>
```

```html
<header class="main-title">About</header>
<app-bio></app-bio>
```

Chapter 14: Certificates Data

14.1 Create It

Create a new folder "data".
Create certificates.data.ts

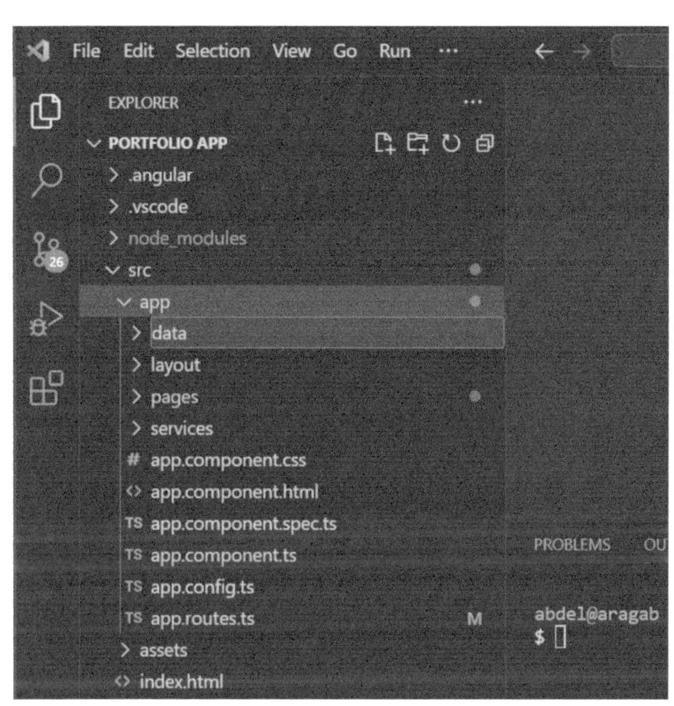

File Edit Selection View Go Run
EXPLORER
PORTFOLIO APP
.angular
.vscode
node_modules
src
app
data
layout
pages
services
app.component.css
app.component.html
app.component.spec.ts
app.component.ts
app.config.ts
app.routes.ts
assets
index.html
PROBLEMS OU
abdel@aragab
$

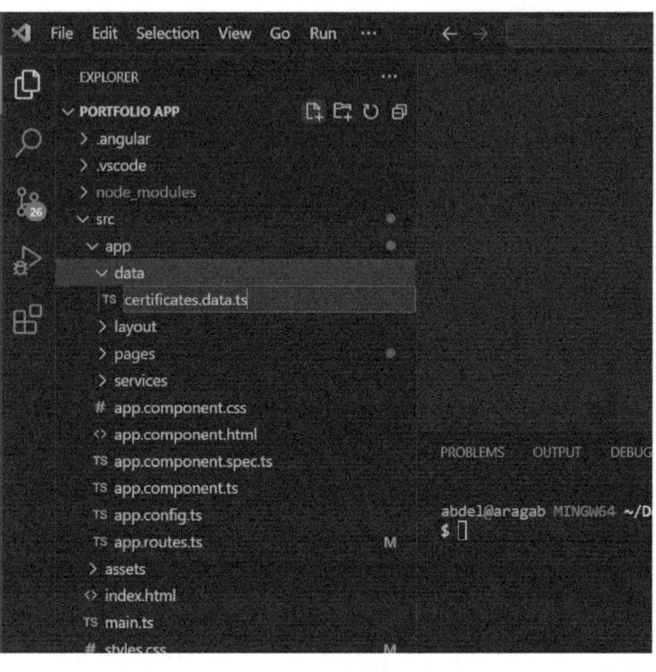

File   Edit   Selection   View   Go   Run   ···
EXPLORER
PORTFOLIO APP
.angular
.vscode
node_modules
src
app
data
certificates.data.ts
layout
pages
services
app.component.css
app.component.html
app.component.spec.ts
app.component.ts
app.config.ts
app.routes.ts   M
assets
index.html
main.ts
styles.css   M
PROBLEMS   OUTPUT   DEBUG
abdel@aragab MINGW64 ~/D
$

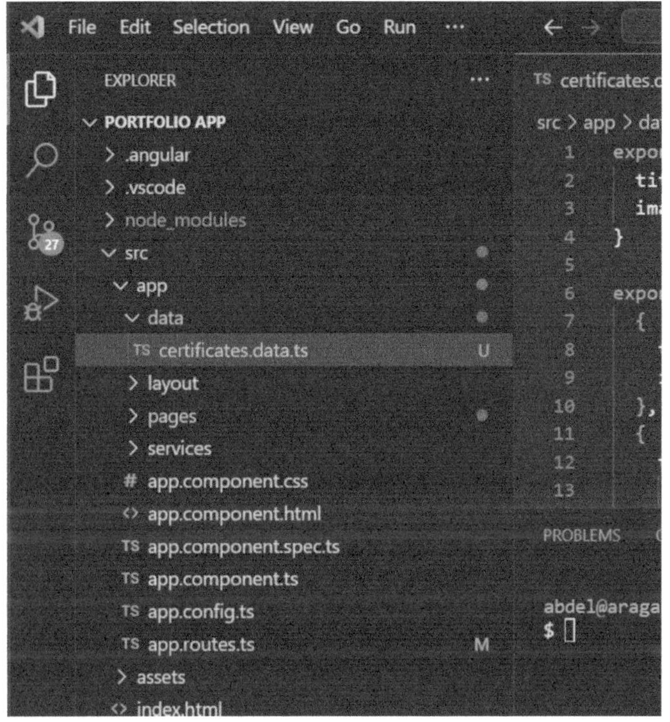

14.2 TS

```ts
export interface Certificate {
  title: string;
  imageUrl: string;
}

export const CERTIFICATES: Certificate[] = [
  {
    title: 'Software Design and Architecture -
University of Alberta',
```

```
    imageUrl:
'assets/images/certificates/architecture.png',
  },
  {
    title:
      'Improve Your English Communication
Skills - Georgia Institute of Technology',
    imageUrl:
'assets/images/certificates/english.png',
  },
  {
    title: 'Microservices Foundations -
LinkedIn',
    imageUrl:
'assets/images/certificates/microservices.png',
  },
  {
    title: 'Ionic - Udemy',
    imageUrl:
'assets/images/certificates/ionic.png',
  },
  {
    title: 'AWS Certified Solutions Architect -
Associate',
    imageUrl:
'assets/images/certificates/aws.png',
  },
  {
    title: 'Oracle Certified Professional, Java
SE 11 Programmer',
    imageUrl:
'assets/images/certificates/java-2.png',
  },
];
```

```typescript
export interface Certificate {
  title: string;
  imageUrl: string;
}

export const CERTIFICATES: Certificate[] = [
  {
    title: 'Software Design and Architecture - University of Alberta',
    imageUrl: 'assets/images/certificates/architecture.png',
  },
  {
    title:
      'Improve Your English Communication Skills - Georgia Institute of Technology',
    imageUrl: 'assets/images/certificates/english.png',
  },
  {
    title: 'Microservices Foundations - LinkedIn',
    imageUrl: 'assets/images/certificates/microservices.png',
  },
  {
    title: 'Ionic - Udemy',
    imageUrl: 'assets/images/certificates/ionic.png',
  },
  {
    title: 'AWS Certified Solutions Architect - Associate',
    imageUrl: 'assets/images/certificates/aws.png',
  },
  {
    title: 'Oracle Certified Professional, Java SE 11 Programmer',
    imageUrl: 'assets/images/certificates/java-2.png',
  },
];
```

Chapter 15: [About] Certificates Component

15.1 Preview

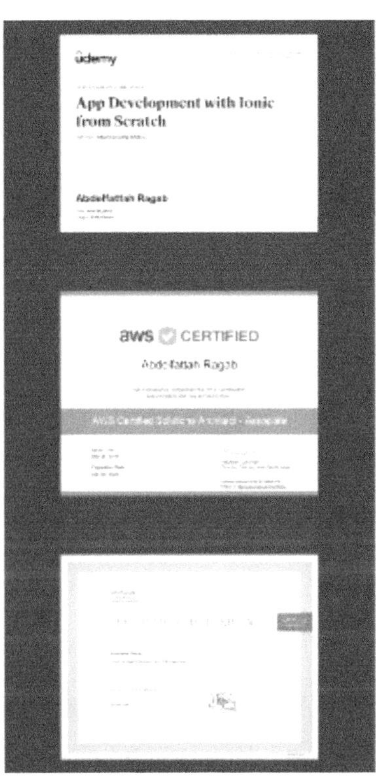

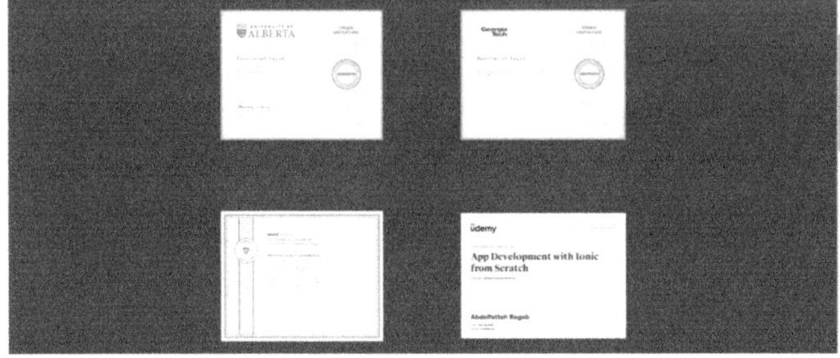

15.2 Create It

```
ng g c pages/about/components/certificates
```

```
abdel@aragab MINGW64 ~/Documents/temp/Portfolio App (master)
$ ng g c pages/about/components/certificates
```

15.3 TS

```typescript
import { Component } from '@angular/core';
import { CERTIFICATES } from
'../../../../data/certificates.data';

@Component({
  selector: 'app-certificates',
  standalone: true,
  imports: [],
  templateUrl: './certificates.component.html',
  styleUrl: './certificates.component.css',
})
export class CertificatesComponent {
  certificates = CERTIFICATES;
}
```

```typescript
import { Component } from '@angular/core';
import { CERTIFICATES } from '../../../../data/certificates.data';

@Component({
  selector: 'app-certificates',
  standalone: true,
  imports: [],
  templateUrl: './certificates.component.html',
  styleUrl: './certificates.component.css',
})
export class CertificatesComponent {
  certificates = CERTIFICATES;
}
```

15.4 HTML

```html
<section class="certificates">
  @for(certificate of certificates; track certificate.title) {
  <img
    [src]="certificate.imageUrl"
    [alt]="certificate.title"
    [title]="certificate.title"
    class="certificate link"
  />
  }
</section>
```

```html
<section class="certificates">
  @for(certificate of certificates; track certificate.title) {
  <img
    [src]="certificate.imageUrl"
    [alt]="certificate.title"
    [title]="certificate.title"
    class="certificate link"
  />
  }
</section>
```

15.5 CSS

```css
.certificates {
  display: grid;
```

```css
  grid-template-columns: 1fr;
  place-items: center center;
  padding: 100px 20px;
  column-gap: 20px;
  row-gap: 60px;
  @media (min-width: 760px) {
    padding: 120px 60px;
    grid-template-columns: 1fr 1fr;
    row-gap: 120px;
  }
}
.certificate {
  width: 300px;
  height: auto;
}
```

```css
1   .certificates {
2     display: grid;
3     grid-template-columns: 1fr;
4     place-items: center center;
5     padding: 100px 20px;
6     column-gap: 20px;
7     row-gap: 60px;
8     @media (min-width: 760px) {
9       padding: 120px 60px;
10      grid-template-columns: 1fr 1fr;
11      row-gap: 120px;
12    }
13  }
14  .certificate {
15    width: 300px;
16    height: auto;
17  }
```

15.6 Use It

```typescript
import { Component } from '@angular/core';
import { BioComponent } from
'./components/bio/bio.component';
```

```typescript
import { CertificatesComponent } from
'./components/certificates/certificates.compone
nt';

@Component({
  selector: 'app-about',
  standalone: true,
  imports: [BioComponent,
CertificatesComponent],
  templateUrl: './about.component.html',
  styleUrl: './about.component.css',
})
export class AboutComponent {}
```

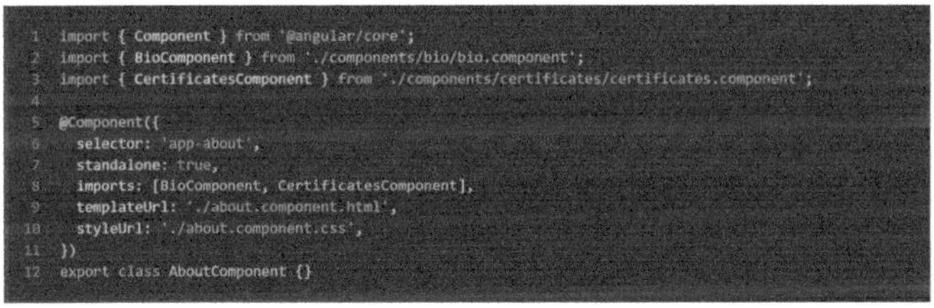

```typescript
1   import { Component } from '@angular/core';
2   import { BioComponent } from './components/bio/bio.component';
3   import { CertificatesComponent } from './components/certificates/certificates.component';
4
5   @Component({
6     selector: 'app-about',
7     standalone: true,
8     imports: [BioComponent, CertificatesComponent],
9     templateUrl: './about.component.html',
10    styleUrl: './about.component.css',
11  })
12  export class AboutComponent {}
```

In about.component.html

```html
<header class="main-title">About</header>
<app-bio></app-bio>
<app-certificates></app-certificates>
```

```html
1   <header class="main-title">About</header>
2   <app-bio></app-bio>
3   <app-certificates></app-certificates>
```

Chapter 16: CV Page

16.1 Preview

- Optimize the complex SQL queries

- Create PDF and Word reports

Senior Software Developer - .NET/Angular

2014 - 2017

Work for clients online:

- Develop the backend system using .NET

- Develop the client side part with Angular

- Search engine optimization

- Copywriting, advertising and marketing

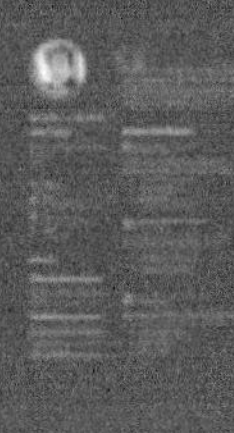

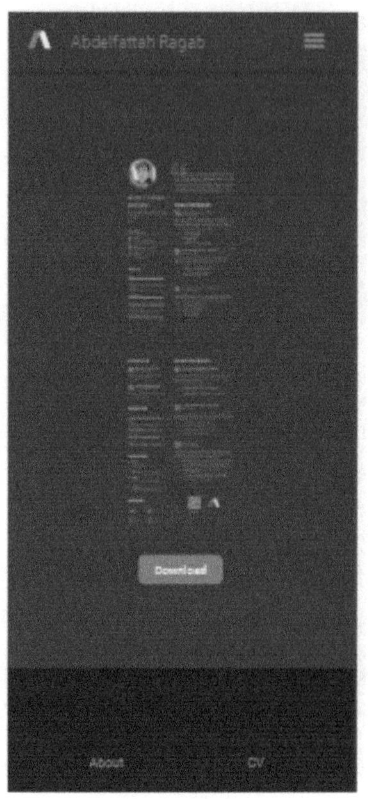
Abdelfattah Ragab
Download
About
CV

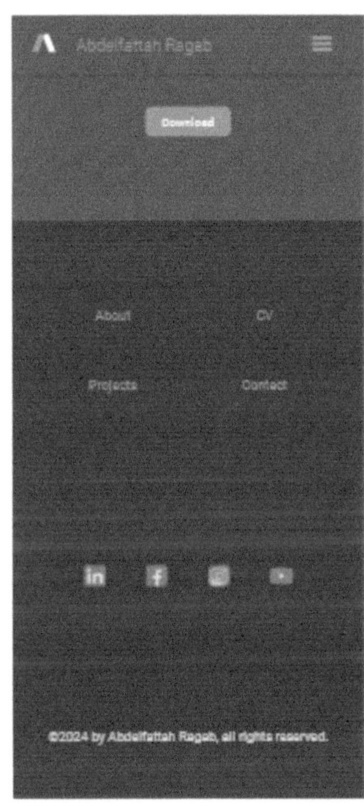
Abdelfattah Ragab
Download
About
CV
Projects
Contact
©2024 by Abdelfattah Ragab, all rights reserved.

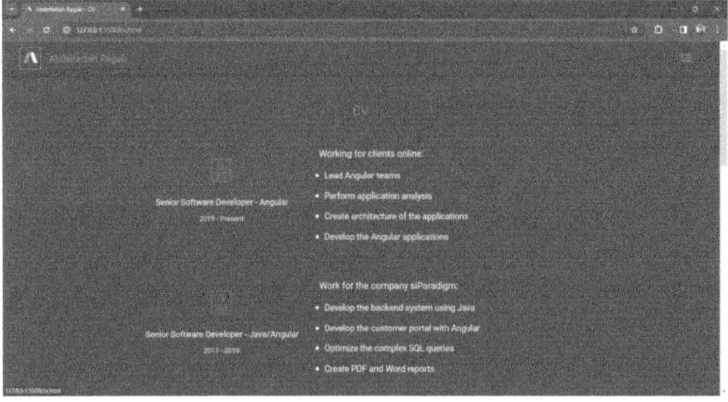
Abdelfattah Ragab - CV
127.0.0.1:5500/cv.html
Abdelfattah Ragab
CV
Working for clients online:
Senior Software Developer - Angular
2019 - Present
Lead Angular teams
Perform application analysis
Create architecture of the applications
Develop the Angular applications
Work for the company siParadigm:
Senior Software Developer - Java/Angular
2017 - 2019
Develop the backend system using Java
Develop the customer portal with Angular
Optimize the complex SQL queries
Create PDF and Word reports
127.0.0.1:5500/cv.html

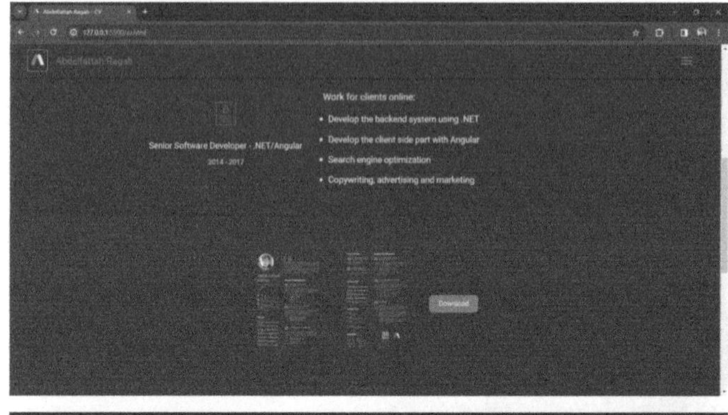

16.2 Page Outline

```
<app-experiences></app-experiences>
<app-download-cv></app-download-cv>
```

16.3 Create It

```
ng g c pages/cv
```

```
abdel@aragab MINGW64 ~/Documents/temp/Portfolio App (master)
$ ng g c pages/cv
```

16.4 Set Title

```
<header class="main-title">CV</header>
```

```
1   <header class="main-title">CV</header>
```

16.5 Add Route

```typescript
import { Routes } from '@angular/router';
import { HomeComponent } from
'./pages/home/home.component';
import { AboutComponent } from
'./pages/about/about.component';
import { CvComponent } from
'./pages/cv/cv.component';

export const routes: Routes = [
  { path: '', redirectTo: 'home', pathMatch:
'full' },
  { path: 'home', component: HomeComponent },
  { path: 'about', component: AboutComponent },
  { path: 'cv', component: CvComponent },
];
```

```typescript
import { Routes } from '@angular/router';
import { HomeComponent } from './pages/home/home.component';
import { AboutComponent } from './pages/about/about.component';

export const routes: Routes = [
  { path: '', redirectTo: 'home', pathMatch: 'full' },
  { path: 'home', component: HomeComponent },
  { path: 'about', component: AboutComponent },
];
```

Chapter 17: Experiences Data

17.1 Create It

In the "data" folder, create experiences.data.ts

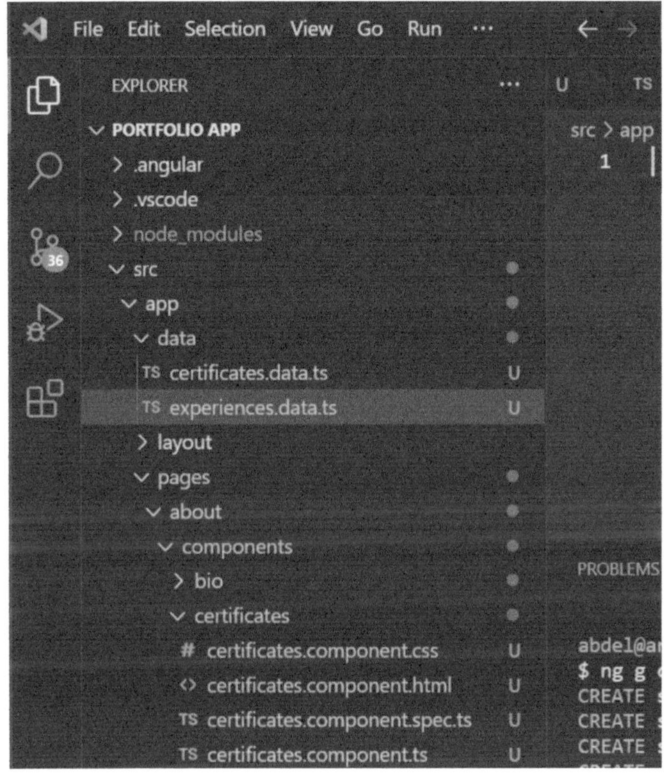

17.2 TS

```ts
export interface Experience {
  title: string;
  subtitle: string;
  linesHeader: string;
  lines: string[];
}

export const EXPERIENCES: Experience[] = [
```

```
  {
    title: 'Senior Software Developer -
Angular',
    subtitle: '2019 - Present',
    linesHeader: 'Working for clients online',
    lines: [
      'Developing and implementing user
interface components',
      'Collaborating with cross-functional
teams to analyze requirements',
      'Designing and implementing scalable and
efficient solutions',
      'Writing clean, maintainable, and
testable code',
    ],
  },
  {
    title: 'Senior Software Developer -
Java/Angular',
    subtitle: '2017 - 2019',
    linesHeader: 'Work for the company
siParadigm',
    lines: [
      'Troubleshooting complex issues in
Angular applications',
      'Conducting code reviews to ensure code
quality and performance',
      'Collaborating with UI/UX designers to
ensure the feasibility',
      'Optimizing application performance by
identifying bottlenecks',
    ],
  },
  {
```

```javascript
    title: 'Senior Software Developer -
.NET/Angular',
    subtitle: '2014 - 2017',
    linesHeader: 'Work for clients online',
    lines: [
      'Integrating third-party libraries and
APIs into Angular applications',
      'Collaborating with backend developers to
design RESTful APIs',
      'Implementing and maintaining unit tests
and end-to-end tests',
      'Participating in Agile development
processes, including sprint planning',
    ],
  },
];
```

```typescript
export interface Experience {
  title: string;
  subtitle: string;
  linesHeader: string;
  lines: string[];
}

export const EXPERIENCES: Experience[] = [
  {
    title: 'Senior Software Developer - Angular',
    subtitle: '2019 - Present',
    linesHeader: 'Working for clients online',
    lines: [
      'Developing and implementing user interface components',
      'Collaborating with cross-functional teams to analyze requirements',
      'Designing and implementing scalable and efficient solutions',
      'Writing clean, maintainable, and testable code',
    ],
  },
  {
    title: 'Senior Software Developer - Java/Angular',
    subtitle: '2017 - 2019',
    linesHeader: 'Work for the company siParadigm',
    lines: [
      'Troubleshooting complex issues in Angular applications',
      'Conducting code reviews to ensure code quality and performance',
      'Collaborating with UI/UX designers to ensure the feasibility',
      'Optimizing application performance by identifying bottlenecks',
    ],
  },
  {
    title: 'Senior Software Developer - .NET/Angular',
    subtitle: '2014 - 2017',
    linesHeader: 'Work for clients online',
    lines: [
      'Integrating third-party libraries and APIs into Angular applications',
      'Collaborating with backend developers to design RESTful APIs',
      'Implementing and maintaining unit tests and end-to-end tests',
      'Participating in Agile development processes, including sprint planning',
    ],
  },
];
```

Chapter 18: [CV] Experiences Component

18.1 Preview

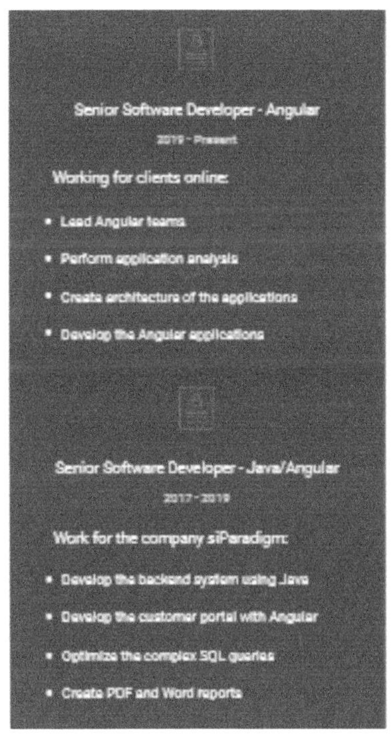

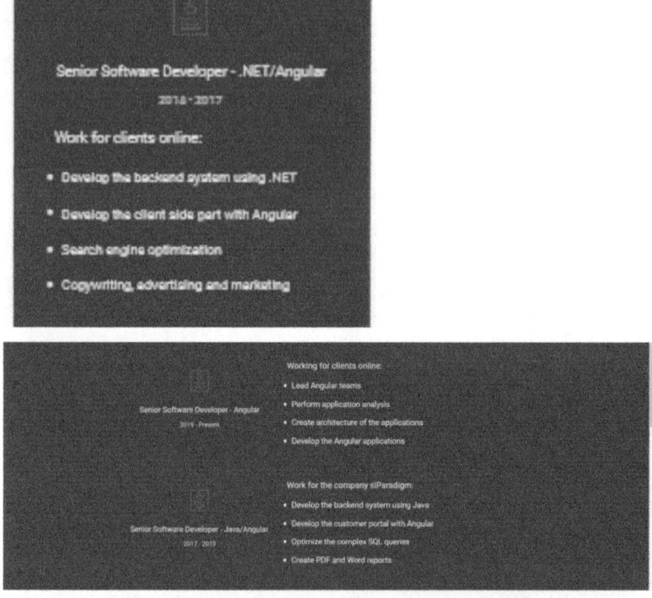

18.2 Create It

```
ng g c pages/cv/components/experiences
```

18.3 TS

```typescript
import { Component } from '@angular/core';
import { EXPERIENCES } from
'../../../../data/experiences.data';

@Component({
  selector: 'app-experiences',
  standalone: true,
  imports: [],
  templateUrl: './experiences.component.html',
  styleUrl: './experiences.component.css',
})
export class ExperiencesComponent {
  experiences = EXPERIENCES;
}
```

```typescript
1   import { Component } from '@angular/core';
2   import { EXPERIENCES } from '../../../../data/experiences.data';
3
4   @Component({
5     selector: 'app-experiences',
6     standalone: true,
7     imports: [],
8     templateUrl: './experiences.component.html',
9     styleUrl: './experiences.component.css',
10  })
11  export class ExperiencesComponent {
12    experiences = EXPERIENCES;
13  }
```

18.4 HTML

```html
@for(experience of experiences; track
experience.title) {
<section class="experience">
  <div class="experience-header">
    <img class="experience-header-icon"
src="assets/images/cv/cv.svg" />
```

```
      <div class="experience-header-title">
        {{ experience.title }}
      </div>
      <div class="experience-header-subtitle">{{
experience.subtitle }}</div>
    </div>
    <div class="experience-content">
      <header>{{ experience.linesHeader
}}</header>
      @for(line of experience.lines; track line)
{
      <span>{{ line }}</span>
      }
    </div>
</section>
}
```

```
1   @for(experience of experiences; track experience.title) {
2     <section class="experience">
3       <div class="experience-header">
4         <img class="experience-header-icon" src="assets/images/cv/cv.svg" />
5         <div class="experience-header-title">
6           {{ experience.title }}
7         </div>
8         <div class="experience-header-subtitle">{{ experience.subtitle }}</div>
9       </div>
10      <div class="experience-content">
11        <header>{{ experience.linesHeader }}</header>
12        @for(line of experience.lines; track line) {
13        <span>{{ line }}</span>
14        }
15      </div>
16    </section>
17  }
```

18.5 CSS

```
.experience {
  display: grid;
  padding: 10px 0px;
  margin-bottom: 40px;
  @media (min-width: 760px) {
    grid-template-columns: 40% 60%;
```

```css
  }
}
.experience-header {
  display: flex;
  flex-direction: column;
  justify-content: center;
  align-items: center;
  gap: 10px;
  margin-top: -30px;
}
.experience-header-icon {
  width: 42px;
  opacity: 0.6;
  margin-bottom: 20px;
}
.experience-header-title {
  font-size: 1.1em;
}
.experience-header-subtitle {
  font-size: 0.9em;
  opacity: 0.8;
}
.experience-content {
  display: flex;
  flex-direction: column;
  justify-content: flex-start;
  align-items: flex-start;
  width: 100%;
  margin-top: 20px;
  @media (min-width: 760px) {
    margin-top: 0px;
  }
}
.experience-content header {
```

```css
    text-align: left;
    font-size: 1.1em;
    margin-bottom: 20px;
    padding-left: 10px;
    @media (min-width: 760px) {
      font-size: 1.2em;
    }
}
.experience-content span {
    font-size: 16px;
    margin: 8px 0px;
    margin-top: -6px;
    width: 100%;
    text-align: left;
    line-height: 40px;
    @media (min-width: 760px) {
      font-size: 18px;
    }
}
.experience-content span::before {
    content: "•";
    margin-right: 10px;
    font-size: 1.8em;
    vertical-align: bottom;
}
```

18.6 Use It

```typescript
import { Component } from '@angular/core';
import { ExperiencesComponent } from
'./components/experiences/experiences.component
';
```

```typescript
@Component({
  selector: 'app-cv',
  standalone: true,
  imports: [ExperiencesComponent],
  templateUrl: './cv.component.html',
  styleUrl: './cv.component.css',
})
export class CvComponent {}
```

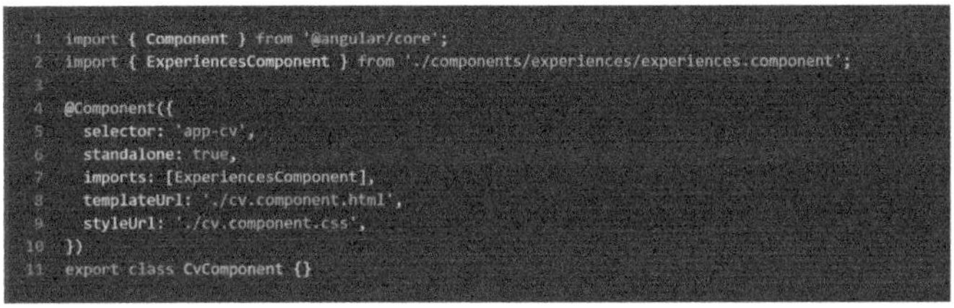

```typescript
1  import { Component } from '@angular/core';
2  import { ExperiencesComponent } from './components/experiences/experiences.component';
3
4  @Component({
5    selector: 'app-cv',
6    standalone: true,
7    imports: [ExperiencesComponent],
8    templateUrl: './cv.component.html',
9    styleUrl: './cv.component.css',
10 })
11 export class CvComponent {}
```

In cv.component.html

```html
<header class="main-title">CV</header>
<app-experiences></app-experiences>
```

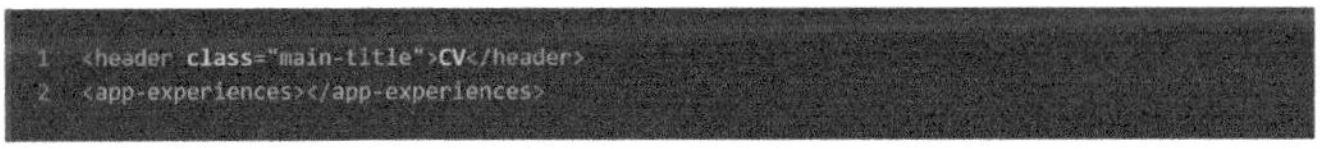

```html
1  <header class="main-title">CV</header>
2  <app-experiences></app-experiences>
```

Chapter 19: [CV] Download CV Component

19.1 Preview

19.2 Create It

```
ng g c pages/cv/components/download-cv
```

```
abdel@aragab MINGW64 ~/Documents/temp/Portfolio App (master)
$ ng g c pages/cv/components/download-cv
```

19.3 TS

No changes.

19.4 HTML

```html
<section class="download-cv">
  <a href="assets/files/cv/Abdelfattah-CV.pdf"
download
    ><img
src="assets/images/cv/Abdelfattah-CV-1.jpg"
class="cv-imagg"
  /></a>
  <a href="assets/files/cv/Abdelfattah-CV.pdf"
download
    ><img
src="assets/images/cv/Abdelfattah-CV-2.jpg"
class="cv-imagg"
  /></a>
  <a href="assets/files/Abdelfattah-CV.pdf"
class="download-button" download>
    Download
  </a>
</section>
```

```html
<section class="download-cv">
  <a href="assets/files/cv/Abdelfattah-CV.pdf" download
    ><img src="assets/images/cv/Abdelfattah-CV-1.jpg" class="cv-imagg"
  /></a>
  <a href="assets/files/cv/Abdelfattah-CV.pdf" download
    ><img src="assets/images/cv/Abdelfattah-CV-2.jpg" class="cv-imagg"
  /></a>
  <a href="assets/files/Abdelfattah-CV.pdf" class="download-button" download>
    Download
  </a>
</section>
```

19.5 CSS

```css
.download-cv {
  display: flex;
  margin-top: 100px;
  column-gap: 30px;
  row-gap: 10px;
  flex-direction: column;
  justify-content: center;
  align-items: center;
  @media (min-width: 760px) {
    flex-direction: row;
  }
}
.cv-imagg {
  width: 160px;
}
.download-button {
  background-color: var(--accent-color-1);
  color: var(--accent-color-2) !important;
  border-radius: 8px;
  padding: 6px 20px;
  font-size: 0.9em;
  margin-top: 6px;
}
```

19.6 Use It

```typescript
import { Component } from '@angular/core';
import { ExperiencesComponent } from
'./components/experiences/experiences.component
';
import { DownloadCvComponent } from
'./components/download-cv/download-cv.component
';

@Component({
  selector: 'app-cv',
  standalone: true,
  imports: [ExperiencesComponent,
DownloadCvComponent],
  templateUrl: './cv.component.html',
  styleUrl: './cv.component.css',
})
export class CvComponent {}
```

```typescript
1   import { Component } from '@angular/core';
2   import { ExperiencesComponent } from './components/experiences/experiences.component';
3   import { DownloadCvComponent } from './components/download-cv/download-cv.component';
4
5   @Component({
6     selector: 'app-cv',
7     standalone: true,
8     imports: [ExperiencesComponent, DownloadCvComponent],
9     templateUrl: './cv.component.html',
10    styleUrl: './cv.component.css',
11  })
12  export class CvComponent {}
```

In cv.component.html

```html
<header class="main-title">CV</header>
<app-experiences></app-experiences>
<app-download-cv></app-download-cv>
```

```html
1   <header class="main-title">CV</header>
2   <app-experiences></app-experiences>
3   <app-download-cv></app-download-cv>
```

Chapter 20: Projects Page

20.1 Preview

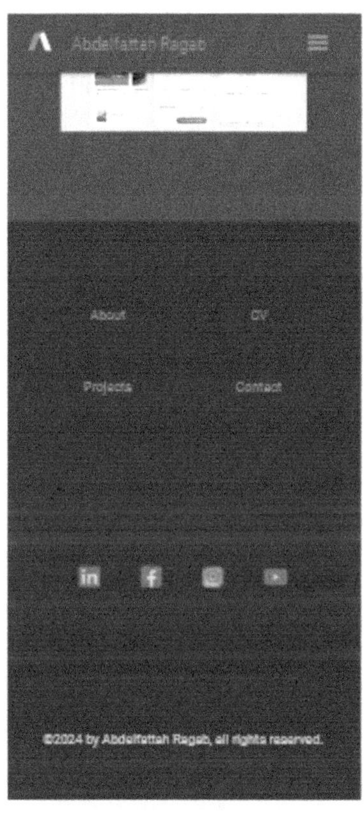
Abdelfattah Ragab
About
CV
Projects
Contact
©2024 by Abdelfattah Ragab, all rights reserved.

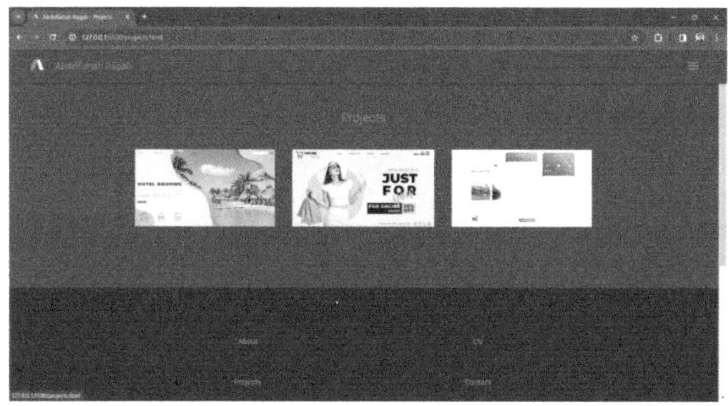
Abdelfattah Ragab - Projects
127.0.0.1:5500/projects.html
Abdelfattah Ragab
Projects
HOTEL BOOKING
JUST FOR
About
CV
Projects
Contact
127.0.0.1:5500/projects.html

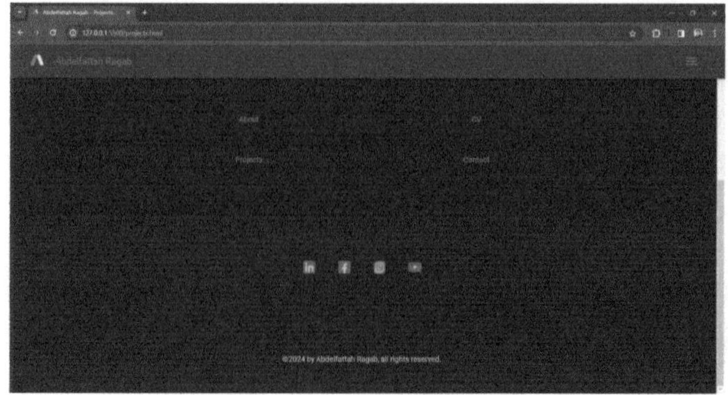

20.2 Page Outline

```
<app-project-gallery></app-project-gallery>
```

20.3 Create It

```
ng g c pages/projects
```

```
abdel@aragab MINGW64 ~/Documents/temp/Portfolio App (master)
$ ng g c pages/projects
```

20.4 Set Title

```
<header class="main-title">Projects</header>
```

```
1   <header class="main-title">Projects</header>
```

20.5 Add Route

```typescript
import { Routes } from '@angular/router';
import { HomeComponent } from
'./pages/home/home.component';
import { AboutComponent } from
'./pages/about/about.component';
import { CvComponent } from
'./pages/cv/cv.component';
import { ProjectsComponent } from
'./pages/projects/projects.component';

export const routes: Routes = [
  { path: '', redirectTo: 'home', pathMatch:
'full' },
  { path: 'home', component: HomeComponent },
  { path: 'about', component: AboutComponent },
  { path: 'cv', component: CvComponent },
  { path: 'projects', component:
ProjectsComponent },
];
```

```typescript
1  import { Routes } from '@angular/router';
2  import { HomeComponent } from './pages/home/home.component';
3  import { AboutComponent } from './pages/about/about.component';
4  import { CvComponent } from './pages/cv/cv.component';
5  import { ProjectsComponent } from './pages/projects/projects.component';
6
7  export const routes: Routes = [
8    { path: '', redirectTo: 'home', pathMatch: 'full' },
9    { path: 'home', component: HomeComponent },
10   { path: 'about', component: AboutComponent },
11   { path: 'cv', component: CvComponent },
12   { path: 'projects', component: ProjectsComponent },
13  ];
```

Chapter 21: Project Gallery Data

21.1 Create It

In the "data" folder, create project-gallery.data.ts

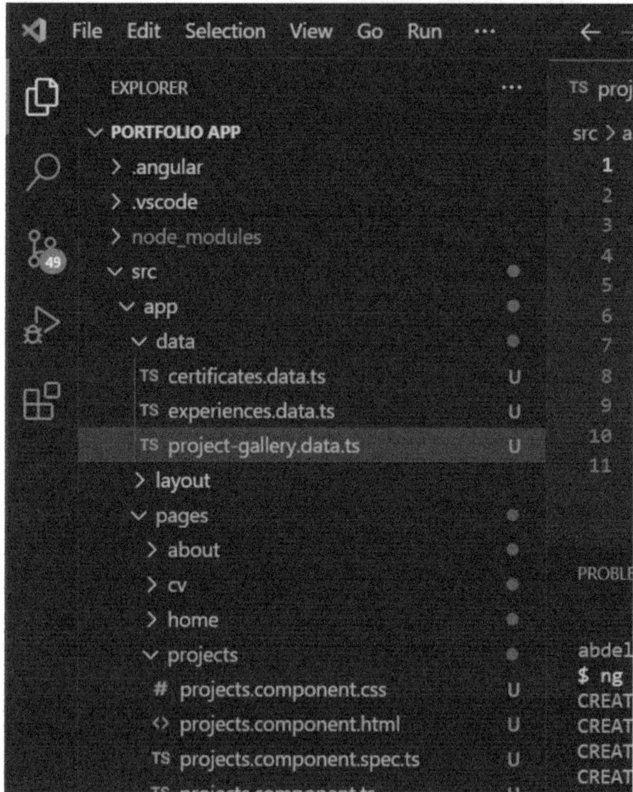

21.2 TS

```
export interface Project {
  title: string;
  imageUrl: string;
}

export const PROJECTS: Project[] = [
  { title: 'Project 1', imageUrl:
'assets/images/projects/project-1.jpg' },
  { title: 'Project 2', imageUrl:
'assets/images/projects/project-2.jpg' },
  { title: 'Project 3', imageUrl:
'assets/images/projects/project-3.jpg' },
];
```

Chapter 22: [Projects] Project Gallery Component

22.1 Preview

22.2 Create It

```
ng g c
pages/projects/components/project-gallery
```

```
abdel@aragab MINGW64 ~/Documents/temp/Portfolio App (master)
$ ng g c pages/projects/components/project-gallery
```

22.3 TS

```typescript
import { Component } from '@angular/core';
import { PROJECTS } from
'../../../../data/project-gallery.data';

@Component({
  selector: 'app-project-gallery',
  standalone: true,
  imports: [],
  templateUrl:
'./project-gallery.component.html',
  styleUrl: './project-gallery.component.css',
})
export class ProjectGalleryComponent {
  projects = PROJECTS;
}
```

```typescript
import { Component } from '@angular/core';
import { PROJECTS } from '../../../../data/project-gallery.data';

@Component({
  selector: 'app-project-gallery',
  standalone: true,
  imports: [],
  templateUrl: './project-gallery.component.html',
  styleUrl: './project-gallery.component.css',
})
export class ProjectGalleryComponent {
  projects = PROJECTS;
}
```

22.4 HTML

```html
<div class="projects">
  @for(project of projects; track
project.title) {
  <img
    [src]="project.imageUrl"
    [alt]="project.title"
    [title]="project.title"
    class="project link"
  />
  }
</div>
```

```html
<div class="projects">
  @for(project of projects; track project.title) {
  <img
    [src]="project.imageUrl"
    [alt]="project.title"
    [title]="project.title"
    class="project link"
  />
  }
</div>
```

22.5 CSS

```css
.projects {
  display: grid;
  gap: 40px;
```

```css
  place-items: center center;
  @media (min-width: 760px) {
    grid-template-columns: repeat(3, 1fr);
    gap: 30px;
  }
}
.project {
  width: 300px;
}
```

```css
1   .projects {
2     display: grid;
3     gap: 40px;
4     place-items: center center;
5     @media (min-width: 760px) {
6       grid-template-columns: repeat(3, 1fr);
7       gap: 30px;
8     }
9   }
10  .project {
11    width: 300px;
12  }
```

22.6 Use It

```typescript
import { Component } from '@angular/core';
import { ProjectGalleryComponent } from
'./components/project-gallery/project-gallery.c
omponent';

@Component({
  selector: 'app-projects',
  standalone: true,
  imports: [ProjectGalleryComponent],
  templateUrl: './projects.component.html',
  styleUrl: './projects.component.css',
})
export class ProjectsComponent {}
```

```typescript
import { Component } from '@angular/core';
import { ProjectGalleryComponent } from './components/project-gallery/project-gallery.component';

@Component({
  selector: 'app-projects',
  standalone: true,
  imports: [ProjectGalleryComponent],
  templateUrl: './projects.component.html',
  styleUrl: './projects.component.css',
})
export class ProjectsComponent {}
```

In projects.component.html

```html
<header class="main-title">Projects</header>
<app-project-gallery></app-project-gallery>
```

Chapter 23: Contact Page

23.1 Preview

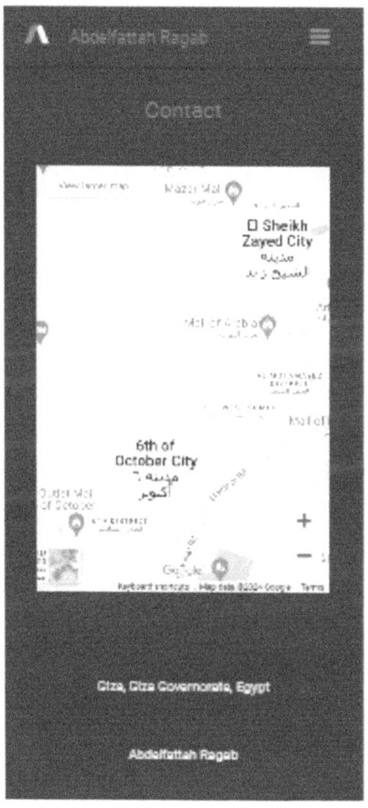

A Abdelfattah Ragab

Keyboard shortcuts   Map data ©2024 Google   Terms

Giza, Giza Governorate, Egypt

Abdelfattah Ragab

+20 11 423 69 630
+20 11 185 06 122

fullstackragab@gmail.com
contact@abdelfattah-ragab.com
sales@abdelfattah-ragab.com

About   CV

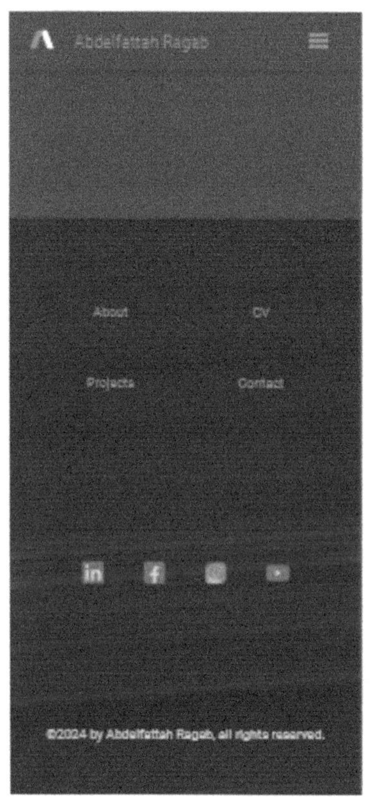
Abdelfattah Ragab
About
CV
Projects
Contact
©2024 by Abdelfattah Ragab, all rights reserved.

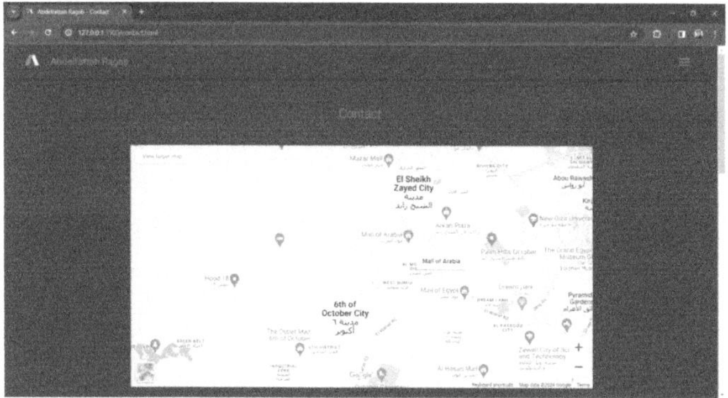
Abdelfattah Ragab - Contact
127.0.0.1:1900/contact
Abdelfattah Ragab
Contact
El Sheikh
Zayed City
مدينة
الشيخ زايد
6th of
October City
مدينة 6
أكتوبر

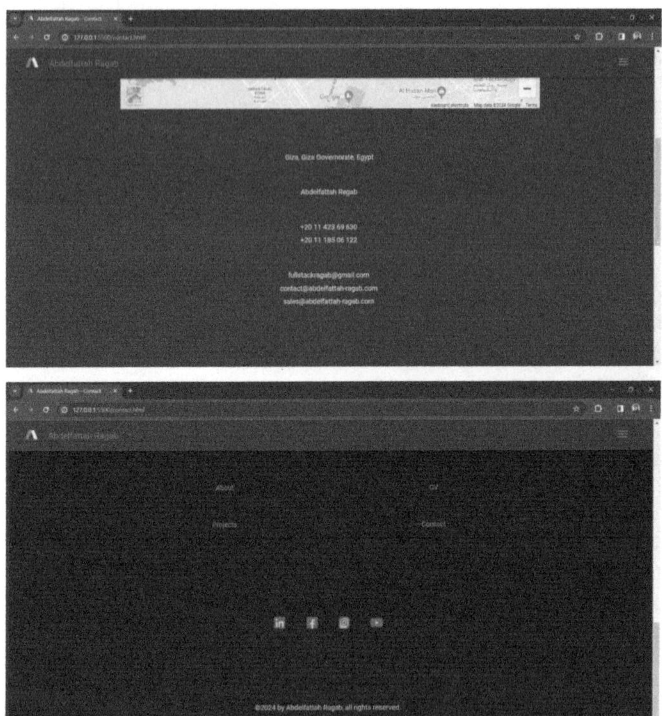

23.2 Page Outline

```
<app-location-map></app-location-map>
<app-contact-info></app-contact-info>
```

23.3 Create It

```
ng g c pages/contact
```

23.4 Set Title

```html
<header class="main-title">Contact</header>
```


23.5 Add Route

```typescript
import { Routes } from '@angular/router';
import { HomeComponent } from
'./pages/home/home.component';
import { AboutComponent } from
'./pages/about/about.component';
import { CvComponent } from
'./pages/cv/cv.component';
import { ProjectsComponent } from
'./pages/projects/projects.component';
import { ContactComponent } from
'./pages/contact/contact.component';

export const routes: Routes = [
  { path: '', redirectTo: 'home', pathMatch:
'full' },
  { path: 'home', component: HomeComponent },
  { path: 'about', component: AboutComponent },
  { path: 'cv', component: CvComponent },
  { path: 'projects', component:
ProjectsComponent },
```

```typescript
  { path: 'contact', component:
ContactComponent },
];
```

```typescript
import { Routes } from '@angular/router';
import { HomeComponent } from './pages/home/home.component';
import { AboutComponent } from './pages/about/about.component';
import { CvComponent } from './pages/cv/cv.component';
import { ProjectsComponent } from './pages/projects/projects.component';
import { ContactComponent } from './pages/contact/contact.component';

export const routes: Routes = [
  { path: '', redirectTo: 'home', pathMatch: 'full' },
  { path: 'home', component: HomeComponent },
  { path: 'about', component: AboutComponent },
  { path: 'cv', component: CvComponent },
  { path: 'projects', component: ProjectsComponent },
  { path: 'contact', component: ContactComponent },
];
```

Chapter 24: [Contact] Location Map Component

24.1 Preview

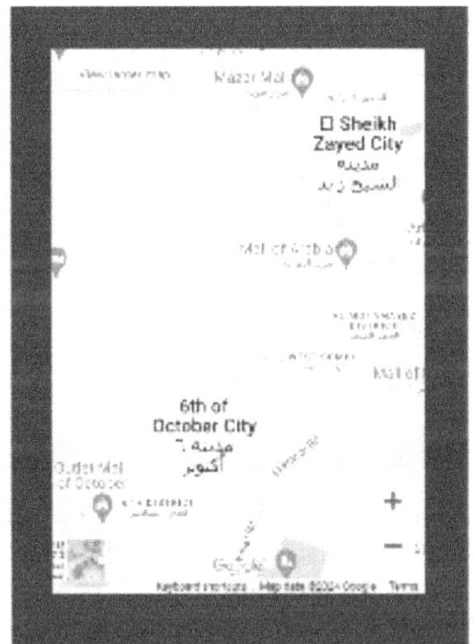

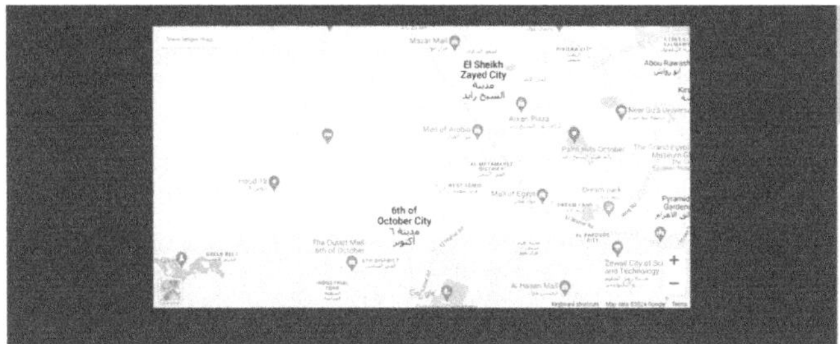

24.2 Create It

```
ng g c pages/contact/components/location-map
```


24.3 TS

No changes.

24.4 HTML

```
<iframe

src="https://www.google.com/maps/embed?pb=!1m14
!1m12!1m3!1d86507.44890895384!2d30.940485229641
485!3d29.9921154773405S3!2m3!1f0!2f0!3f0!3m2!1i
1024!2i768!4f13.1!5e0!3m2!1sen!2seg!4v167959642
4897!5m2!1sen!2seg"
  class="map"
  allowfullscreen=""
  loading="lazy"
  referrerpolicy="no-referrer-when-downgrade"
></iframe>
```

24.5 CSS

```css
.map {
  border: 0;
  background-image:
url(/assets/images/other/loading.gif);
  background-repeat: no-repeat;
  background-size: 50px 50px;
  background-position: center top;
  width: 100%;
  height: 500px;
}
```

```css
1  .map {
2    border: 0;
3    background-image: url(/assets/images/other/loading.gif);
4    background-repeat: no-repeat;
5    background-size: 50px 50px;
6    background-position: center top;
7    width: 100%;
8    height: 500px;
9  }
```

24.6 Use It

```typescript
import { Component } from '@angular/core';
import { LocationMapComponent } from
'./components/location-map/location-map.compone
nt';

@Component({
  selector: 'app-contact',
  standalone: true,
  imports: [LocationMapComponent],
  templateUrl: './contact.component.html',
  styleUrl: './contact.component.css',
})
```

```
export class ContactComponent {}
```

```typescript
1   import { Component } from '@angular/core';
2   import { LocationMapComponent } from './components/location-map/location-map.component';
3
4   @Component({
5     selector: 'app-contact',
6     standalone: true,
7     imports: [LocationMapComponent],
8     templateUrl: './contact.component.html',
9     styleUrl: './contact.component.css',
10  })
11  export class ContactComponent {}
```

In contact.component.html

```html
<header class="main-title">Contact</header>
<app-location-map></app-location-map>
```

```html
1   <header class="main-title">Contact</header>
2   <app-location-map></app-location-map>
```

Chapter 25: [Contact] Contact Info Component

25.1 Preview

25.2 Create It

```
ng g c pages/contact/components/contact-info
```

25.3 TS

No changes.

25.4 HTML

```html
<section class="contact-info">
  <p>Giza, Giza Governorate, Egypt</p>
  <p>Abdelfattah Ragab</p>
  <p>
    +20 11 423 69 630
    <br />
    +20 11 185 06 122
  </p>
  <p>
    fullstackragab&#64;gmail.com
    <br />
    contact&#64;abdelfattah-ragab.com
    <br />
    sales&#64;abdelfattah-ragab.com
  </p>
</section>
```

```html
<section class="contact-info">
  <p>Giza, Giza Governorate, Egypt</p>
  <p>Abdelfattah Ragab</p>
  <p>
    +20 11 423 69 630
    <br />
    +20 11 185 06 122
  </p>
  <p>
    fullstackragab&#64;gmail.com
    <br />
    contact&#64;abdelfattah-ragab.com
    <br />
    sales&#64;abdelfattah-ragab.com
  </p>
</section>
```

25.5 CSS

```css
.contact-info {
  padding: 40px 0px;
}
.contact-info p {
  margin: 50px 0px;
  line-height: 30px;
  text-align: center;
}
```

```css
.contact-info {
  padding: 40px 0px;
}
.contact-info p {
  margin: 50px 0px;
  line-height: 30px;
  text-align: center;
}
```

25.6 Use It

```typescript
import { Component } from '@angular/core';
import { LocationMapComponent } from
'./components/location-map/location-map.compone
nt';
```

```typescript
import { ContactInfoComponent } from
'./components/contact-info/contact-info.compone
nt';

@Component({
  selector: 'app-contact',
  standalone: true,
  imports: [LocationMapComponent,
ContactInfoComponent],
  templateUrl: './contact.component.html',
  styleUrl: './contact.component.css',
})
export class ContactComponent {}
```

```typescript
import { Component } from '@angular/core';
import { LocationMapComponent } from './components/location-map/location-map.component';
import { ContactInfoComponent } from './components/contact-info/contact-info.component';

@Component({
  selector: 'app-contact',
  standalone: true,
  imports: [LocationMapComponent, ContactInfoComponent],
  templateUrl: './contact.component.html',
  styleUrl: './contact.component.css',
})
export class ContactComponent {}
```

In contact.component.html

```html
<header class="main-title">Contact</header>
<app-location-map></app-location-map>
<app-contact-info></app-contact-info>
```

```html
<header class="main-title">Contact</header>
<app-location-map></app-location-map>
<app-contact-info></app-contact-info>
```

Conclusion

Congratulations! You have completed the book "Angular Portfolio App Development: Create Your Personal Brand". Now you have a comprehensive understanding of the powerful CSS Multi-Column layout. Remember that learning is an ongoing process. Practice makes perfect — build your own projects, experiment with the features you learn, and delve into the extensive online resources.

Thank you for joining me in my exploration of CSS Multi-Column layout. I wish you the best of luck on your programming journey. Have fun programming and good luck with your applications!

Media Attribution

Stylish successful woman pointing left and smiling
Image by cookie_studio on Freepik

Watercolor paper texture
Image by kues1 on Freepik

Free photo modern luxury bedroom suite and bathroom
Image by dit26978 on Freepik

Luxury golden flat badges set
Image by pch.vector on Freepik

Free vector modern hotel landing page template with photo
Image by Freepik

Free PSD landing page for online fashion sale
Image by Freepik

Travel booking app
Image by pikisuperstar on Freepik

Books - Abdelfattah Ragab

Register your free account on the author's website to receive discounts, offers and the latest information.

https://books.abdelfattah-ragab.com/

Also by Abdelfattah Ragab

- ◇ Angular Portfolio App Development
- ◇ Responsive Layouts: Flex, Grid and Multi-Column
- ◇ Angular Shopping Store
- ◇ Shrova Mall
- ◇ Stripe Integration in Angular

About the Author

Abdelfattah Ragab is a professional software developer
with more than 20 years of experience.
https://abdelfattah-ragab.com

About the Publisher

Abdelfattah Ragab is a highly qualified and experienced software developer with over 20 years of experience in the industry. Specializing in front-end development, Abdelfattah Ragab has a deep understanding of Angular, JavaScript, TypeScript, HTML and CSS. Read more at https://abdelfattah-ragab.com

Zeitfracht Medien GmbH
Ferdinand-Jühlke-Straße 7,
99095 - DE, Erfurt
produktsicherheit@zeitfracht.de